Gendering the Massification Generation

Gendering the Massification Generation examines why young people from the same families and communities in India experience different decision-making processes regarding higher education access because of their gender. In India and other contexts where higher education is massifying, and gender parity of enrolment has been achieved at the undergraduate level, there are still many questions to be asked about gender and access to higher education. Based on an exploratory study of gendered higher education access and choice within the state of Haryana, India, the authors explore the gender inequalities of higher education access and choice in the Indian context and connect these with the broader international phenomenon of widening participation.

Through an in-depth analysis of the 'massification generation', where young people from relatively disadvantaged backgrounds are accessing higher education, often for the first time in their families and communities, readers are encouraged to apply a lens of social disadvantage and gender and to recognise the norms and transgressions of femininity and masculinity in relation to higher education access and choice.

With global implications for the ways in which gender is analysed and framed in widening participation research and policy, this is the ideal book for scholars, students and policy makers working on higher education, as well as for researchers and NGOs specialising in gender, school-to-higher education transitions, international development, sociology and area studies.

Emily F. Henderson is Reader in Gender and International Higher Education, Department of Education Studies, and Director of the Doctoral Education and Academia Research Centre, University of Warwick, Coventry, United Kingdom. She is also Visiting Professor at the Centre for Policy Research in Higher Education, National Institute of Educational Planning and Administration, New Delhi, India.

Nidhi S. Sabharwal is Associate Professor at the Centre for Policy Research in Higher Education, National Institute of Educational Planning and Administration, India, and is Honorary Associate Professor in the Department of Education Studies at the University of Warwick, United Kingdom.

Anjali Thomas is an early career researcher, recently holding post-doctoral roles at the University of Warwick on the 'Fair Chance for Education' project and University of Liverpool; she holds a PhD from Department of Education Studies, University of Warwick, United Kingdom (funded by WCPRS and Fair Chance Foundation).

Julie Mansuy is Founder and Director of Active4Research Ltd. and was the 'Fair Chance for Education' Project Research Coordinator and holds a PhD from the Law School, University of Warwick, United Kingdom.

Ann Stewart is Professor of Law in the Law School, University of Warwick, United Kingdom, and previously Visiting Research Professor, Centre for Law and Governance, Jawaharlal Nehru University, New Delhi, India.

Sharmila Rathee is Assistant Professor at the Department of Elementary Education, University of Delhi, India, and a Recipient of the American Disability Act Inclusive Education Fellowship.

Renu Yadav is Associate Professor in the Department of Teacher Education, Central University of Haryana, Mahendragarh, Haryana, India. She is also Convenor of the Women's Empowerment Cell and Deputy Dean of Students' Welfare.

Nikita Samanta is a PhD researcher in Gender and Education at the University of Warwick Law School, funded by WCPRS and Fair Chance Foundation.

Gendering the Massification Generation
Higher Education Access and Choice in India

**Emily F. Henderson,
Nidhi S. Sabharwal,
Anjali Thomas, Julie Mansuy,
Ann Stewart, Sharmila Rathee,
Renu Yadav and Nikita Samanta**

LONDON AND NEW YORK

First published 2024
by Routledge
4 Park Square, Milton Park, Abingdon, Oxon OX14 4RN

and by Routledge
605 Third Avenue, New York, NY 10158

Routledge is an imprint of the Taylor & Francis Group, an informa business

© 2024 Emily F. Henderson, Nidhi S. Sabharwal, Anjali Thomas, Julie Mansuy, Ann Stewart, Sharmila Rathee, Renu Yadav and Nikita Samanta

The right of Emily F. Henderson, Nidhi S. Sabharwal, Anjali Thomas, Julie Mansuy, Ann Stewart, Sharmila Rathee, Renu Yadav and Nikita Samanta to be identified as authors of this work has been asserted in accordance with sections 77 and 78 of the Copyright, Designs and Patents Act 1988.

All rights reserved. No part of this book may be reprinted or reproduced or utilised in any form or by any electronic, mechanical, or other means, now known or hereafter invented, including photocopying and recording, or in any information storage or retrieval system, without permission in writing from the publishers.

Trademark notice: Product or corporate names may be trademarks or registered trademarks, and are used only for identification and explanation without intent to infringe.

British Library Cataloguing-in-Publication Data
A catalogue record for this book is available from the British Library

ISBN: 978-1-032-36300-4 (hbk)
ISBN: 978-1-032-36301-1 (pbk)
ISBN: 978-1-003-33121-6 (ebk)

DOI: 10.4324/9781003331216

This book is dedicated to trailblazing young people in Haryana, across India and worldwide, who transgress gender norms in carving out their own futures and thus make the way easier for others following in their footsteps.

This book is also dedicated to Prem Chowdhry, whose nuanced, incisive and wide-ranging scholarship on gender in Haryana vastly enriched our work.

Contents

Acknowledgements   ix
List of tables and figures   x
List of abbreviations   xi
Glossary   xiii

1 Introduction to Gendering the Massification Generation   1
   1.1 *Introduction 1*
   1.2 *Higher education in India 2*
   1.3 *Gender and higher education in India 7*
   1.4 *Analytical approach to gendering the massification generation 10*
   1.5 *Haryana 12*
   1.6 *The empirical study 15*
   1.7 *Navigating this book 16*
   References 17

2 The massification generation   21
   2.1 *Introduction 21*
   2.2 *Previous generations – education and employment 22*
   2.3 *The massification generation 29*
   2.4 *Conclusion 36*
   References 38

3 Gendering the massification generation   40
   3.1 *Introduction 40*
   3.2 *Gendering previous generations – education and employment 41*

3.3 Gendering the massification generation 49
3.4 Conclusion 53
References 55

4 Honour and marriage: femininity and higher education access 57
4.1 Introduction 57
4.2 Honour and safety – higher education as risk for young women 58
4.3 Higher education and marriage 67
4.4 Conclusion 76
References 77

5 Family responsibility: masculinity and higher education access 80
5.1 Introduction 80
5.2 Family responsibility – higher education as risk for young men 81
5.3 Conclusion 94
References 96

6 Conclusion 98
6.1 Introduction 98
6.2 Gendering the massification generation 99
6.3 Implications for policy strategy and further research 101
6.4 Furthering gender analysis of higher education access and choice 103
6.5 Final thoughts 104
References 104

Appendix A: The 'Fair Chance for Education' project 105
Appendix B: Details of the participants and survey sample 108
   Participant information for the qualitative study 108
   Survey sample information 110
   Further particulars on the study procedure and data analysis 111
Index 112

Acknowledgements

The authors would like to thank the funders of the 'A Fair Chance for Education: Gendered Pathways to Educational Success in Haryana' project (www.warwick.ac.uk/haryana) including primarily the Fair Chance Foundation, in addition to Warwick Collaborative Postgraduate Research Scholarship, Department of Education Studies, the School of Law, and additional contributions from the University of Warwick's donor community.

In addition to the authors of this book, many colleagues contributed their thoughts and advice to the research that underpins this book, including Ian Abbott; Nandini Manjrekar and Manish Jain; N. M. Varghese and other colleagues at NIEPA; the project's Research Advisory Group: Kiran Bhatty, Farida Khan, Pankaj Mittal, Claire Noronha, Ratna Sudarshan, Asha Singh; the project's Consultative Group (in addition to book authors Sharmila Rathee and Renu Yadav): Manika Bora, Rachna Chaudhary, Parimala Doss, Lovitoli Jimo, Anima Mali, Shubhra Nagalia, Kamlesh Narwana, Manju Panwar, Alka Shah, Roma Smart Joseph, Anjali Tiwari, Laksh Venkataraman. The following colleagues also contributed to the research work: Denise Chew and Marian Tachibana (literature review database); Sooraj H. S., Annu Kumari, Sohan Lal (data collection); Somak Biswas (transcription). The authors express sincere gratitude to those who read draft work and provided invaluable feedback: Vincent Benezech, John Henderson, Karen Henderson, Ragini Khurana, S. Arokia Mary, Denisse Lillo Sierra, Rebecca Welsh and, in particular, Holly Henderson.

Finally, the book would never have come to be without the colleges who participated in the study, including the staff who were so generous with their time in facilitating the data collection and participating in interviews, and the students who provided such rich insights into their educational experiences and trajectories.

Tables and figures

Figures

1.1	A Government College in Haryana	6
1.2	A Government College Classroom in Haryana	7
2.1	A Village in Haryana	31
2.2	A Village Home in Haryana	32
2.3	Share of Schooling That Is Private by Level of Schooling and College	35
3.1	Grandparents' Educational Attainment by the Gender of Grandparent, across the Three Sampled Colleges	44
3.2	Incidence of Zero Formal Education Compared by Mothers and Fathers and Caste Group, across the Three Sampled Colleges	45
3.3	Proportion of Students Who Attended Private School by Level of Education and Gender, across All Three Sampled Colleges	52
4.1	The Grounds of a Government College in Haryana	65

Tables

A.1	Student Interview Participant Basic Information	108
A.2	Student FGD Participant Basic Information	109
A.3	College Representative Interviews Participant Basic Information	109
A.4	Survey Sample Information: By College and Overall	110

Abbreviations

ASER	Annual Status of Education Report
BA	Bachelor of Arts
BCA	Backward Classes A (Haryana designation for part of the Backward Classes section)
BCB	Backward Classes B (Haryana designation for part of the Backward Classes section)
BCom	Bachelor of Commerce
BEd	Bachelor of Education
BSc	Bachelor of Sciences
CPRHE	Centre for Policy Research in Higher Education
DEd	Diploma of Education
EWS	Economically Weaker Sections (official designation)
FGD	Focus Group Discussion
GER	Gross Enrolment Ratio
GPI	Gender Parity Index
IIT	Indian Institutes of Technology
JBT	Junior Basic Training
MA	Master of Arts
MBBS	Bachelor of Medicine, Bachelor of Surgery
MCom	Masters of Commerce
MDC	Mahendragarh District College (college pseudonym)
MHRD	Ministry of Human Resource Development
MoE	Ministry of Education
MoI	Medium of Instruction
NCC	National Cadet Corps (the youth wing of the Indian Armed Forces)
NCR	National Capital Region
n.d.	No date
NEP	National Education Policy
NIEPA	National Institute of Educational Planning and Administration (formerly NUEPA)
NSO	National Statistical Office
NSSO	National Sample Survey Organisation

NUEPA	National University of Educational Planning and Administration (former name of NIEPA)
OBC	Other Backward Classes (official designation)
PLFS	Periodic Labour Force Survey
RTE	Right to Education
SC	Scheduled Castes (official designation)
SDC	Sonipat District College (college pseudonym)
SiDC	Sirsa District College (college pseudonym)
ST	Scheduled Tribes (official designation)
UGC	University Grants Committee
WCD	Women and Child Development
WPR	Workforce Participation Rate

Glossary

bahar	outside
Beti Bachao, Beti Padhao	'Save the girl child, educate the girl child' (campaign)
dada	paternal grandfather
dadi	paternal grandmother
gobar ke uple	dung fuel cakes
gotra	a term designating lineage along caste lines
izzat	honour
mahaul	environment
nana	maternal grandfather
nani	maternal grandmother
sasural	marital home, that is household including in-laws
scooty	two-wheeled vehicle, e.g. Moped or Vesper

1 Introduction to *Gendering the Massification Generation*

1.1 Introduction

Why do young people from the same families and communities experience different decision-making processes about their educational futures? Why are different gendered decisions taken about applying for higher education? Gender inequalities persist even when the equal enrolment of genders in higher education has been achieved – for instance relating to the choice of institution and subject. These gendered choices are rooted in long-standing dominant codes of masculinity and femininity which determine what the purpose of higher education is understood to be, and whether higher education is seen to be an appropriate choice. This book explores gender inequalities of higher education access and choice in India and situates the Indian context within the international research on widening participation. Based on an exploratory study of gendered higher education access and choice in the state of Haryana, India (see Appendix A), the focus of the book is the *massification generation* in India, where young people from relatively disadvantaged backgrounds are accessing higher education in greater numbers, often as the first people to do so in their families and communities.

The Indian higher education system is highly complex and multifaceted. The sector is expanding at a rapid rate and involves mass privatisation. This expansion of the private sector influences the direction of India's higher education massification, which means that the massification is weighted towards the middle classes and more privileged caste groups (Varghese et al., 2019). At the same time, huge numbers of young people from relatively disadvantaged backgrounds are applying to higher education, with government colleges being popular destinations. Government colleges are relatively low-cost, locally situated higher education providers (Tierney & Sabharwal, 2016), and as such they attract young people who would not otherwise be in a position to enrol in higher education.

India has attained gender parity (equal numbers of women and men students) of enrolment at the undergraduate level (MHRD, 2019). This has led to the suggestion that gender inequalities in higher education are 'solved', with

DOI: 10.4324/9781003331216-1

other social inequalities appearing more pressing – a situation which is not limited to India (Leathwood & Read, 2009). However, this focus on parity leads to concerning oversimplifications of the ways in which gender impacts upon young people's educational trajectories. This book takes a stand within these debates, as we argue that gender inequality is still playing out, even among young people who successfully enter higher education, and that gender impacts upon the choices and possibilities that shape young people's higher education decisions and therefore their life paths. A core aim of the volume is to develop a gender lens that captures the nuances of gender where it meets higher education access and choice, which may be applied across and beyond the Indian context.

The gender lens explores how gendered codes of masculinity and femininity influence how young people make decisions about their futures – and how decisions are made for young people by other gendered individuals in their families and communities (Henderson et al., 2024). The gender lens also seeks to identify transgression of gender norms, arguing that transformation often takes the form of transgression in its initial stages. The overarching aim of the book is to explore *how young people from the same relatively disadvantaged families and communities in India experience higher education access and choice differently because of their gender* – and how these gender issues may be theorised in order to understand the gendered dynamics of other higher education contexts in India and beyond.

This introductory chapter lays out the foundations for the book. First, the Indian higher education context is introduced, including setting the scene for the massification of higher education and the nature of government colleges. The chapter then sets out the key themes covered by the research field of gender and higher education access and choice. Following on from these sections, the conceptualisation of gender that is employed in the book is introduced. The chapter then sets out the specific context that lies at the heart of the book: the state of Haryana in North India. Haryana is introduced in terms of its contextual specificities, prevalent gender norms and higher education provision. The empirical study that underpins the book is introduced in the next section. Finally, the structure of the chapters to follow is laid out.

1.2 Higher education in India

Higher education in India is framed with intertwined historical narratives. There have been higher institutes of learning in India for many centuries, and this long history of high culture and learning is embedded in current framings of higher education in India, including in the most recent policy at the time of writing, National Education Policy (NEP) 2020 (MHRD, 2020). At the same time, during the British colonial era, a version of the British higher education system was imposed upon India, with the aim of creating a class of educated workers to serve the British rule (Ghosh, 1995). Hallmarks of the colonial legacy are the affiliated college system which resembles the collegiate system

Introduction to Gendering the Massification Generation 3

that is associated with Oxford and Cambridge in the UK, a prescriptive curriculum and mode of delivery and a strong tendency towards bureaucratic processes. These narratives intertwine in discussions of how higher education in India should develop in the modern era – how to create not only a higher education system that embraces the cultural roots of higher learning in India but also a system that stretches beyond the restrictions of the colonial legacy – a system that is not only nationally appropriate but also globally competitive.

A third narrative framing Indian higher education characterises the post-Independence period from 1947 onwards, where empowering marginalised groups was taken up as a constitutional priority (Deshpande, 2013). In India, the caste system, which is a long-standing social stratification system that was exacerbated during the British colonial period, is still prevalent. This sociocultural system differentiates between family lines as belonging to different social strata by birth, and traditionally the different strata were characterised by the profession to be undertaken by that family line, with the more erudite and 'noble' professions being higher caste and the menial and tasks designated as 'unclean' being completed by lower caste groups or so-called 'untouchable' groups, now known as Dalits. Social stigma and discrimination are still associated with lower caste groups and Dalits, and these groups often face greater levels of socio-economic disadvantage (Borooah et al., 2015). Along with those who are marginalised within the caste system, there are also indigenous groups known legally as 'tribes' or as Adivasis which were also disadvantaged during the British rule and which face many challenges in terms of accessing education and basic services, especially those groups that are located in remote areas (Banerjee, 2016). Religious minorities have also been singled out for attention. Muslim communities in particular face issues of social marginalisation in India (Ansari, 2018). Women's access to education has also been facilitated through policy initiatives to improve the access to education. We discuss the policy initiatives that have been implemented to open up the Indian higher education further later in the chapter, but this brief introduction to the specific axes of inequality operating in Indian society serves to demonstrate that the third narrative framing – empowering marginalised groups to enter and succeed in higher education – is a complex and multifaceted framing which characterises many debates about the future of higher education in India.

Indian higher education has witnessed a significant expansion in recent decades. Traditionally an exclusive domain of the elite, India entered a stage of massification in the 21st century. The Gross Enrolment Ratio (GER) at the undergraduate level moved from the elite stage in the 1990s (<10%) to a GER of 27.1% in 2020 (MoE, 2020). The system is now the second largest in the world after China. The Indian higher education system is complex, with several different types of institutions and different governance structures.[1] Higher education institutions can be broadly categorised across multiple dimensions such as government, private-aided (i.e. a private institution which is in part supported by a government grant, also known as government-aided) and private colleges; central, state and private universities; deemed universities, open universities and special institutions of national importance such as the Indian Institutes of Technology (IITs). Universities are the main institutional form of higher education, and they often have affiliated colleges which are government, government-aided or private; these colleges deliver the majority of undergraduate education in India. In terms of the sheer scale of the system, in 2020, there were almost 40,000 colleges. While a majority of colleges are private institutions, these colleges serve less than half of the total enrolled students within the college sector. On the other hand, government colleges, which comprise just over 20% of the total number of colleges, serve more than a third of the student population; the state system is, as a result, under significant strain.

As noted earlier, one of the main characteristics of the massification of Indian higher education, and indeed a partial explanation of the sheer number of institutions, is the reliance on the private sector (Panigrahi, 2020). The expansion of higher education in India has largely been achieved through the founding of higher education institutions by the private sector and the offering of self-financing courses (i.e. courses which are not government-subsidised) in public higher education institutions (Varghese, 2015). Importantly, private institutions are not, at the time of writing, bound by the same affirmative action policies as state-funded institutions. The expense and lack of affirmative action structures associated with private education mean that Indian higher education, despite reaching a massification stage statistically speaking, is stratified in terms of who can access which institutions and which courses.

Alongside privatisation, as a major characteristic of the Indian higher education system, is affirmative action. As discussed earlier, Independence-era India was particularly concerned with empowering marginalised groups, and the Constitution was developed with affirmative action clearly embedded within its framework. The Constitution includes a categorisation of marginalised groups, setting out lists of lower caste groups as 'Other Backward Classes' (OBC), former untouchable groups as 'Scheduled Castes' (SC) and indigenous groups as 'Scheduled Tribes' (ST). These lists and designations (which have some variety within individual states) are then used as the basis for the reservation system, which is a quota system deployed across the public sector. Within higher education, these quotas or 'reservations' apply to state-funded and government-aided institutions in terms of student admissions – reserving places or 'seats' for marginalised groups – as well as reservations for the appointment of staff.[2] In addition to the reservation system, affirmative action measures to overcome barriers to higher education entry have taken the form of relaxation in entry requirements, scholarships, fee concessions and accommodation in student hostels. Strategies to promote equity in access in the most recent policy, NEP 2020 (MHRD, 2020), include maintaining the reservation policy for admission to public higher education institutions. NEP 2020 encourages the state and higher education institutions to extend financial support in the form of subsidised tuition fees, scholarships and student accommodation facilities for students from disadvantaged social groups in order to boost enrolment. Finally, it is important to note that interventions in lower levels of schooling have contributed to the expansion of higher education access in India; India has achieved near-universal primary enrolment and a vast improvement in higher secondary enrolments primarily due to initiatives such as publicly funded programmes at the primary level and the passing of the Right to Education (RTE) Act in 2002.

The Indian higher education system, as we have described it so far, is in a period of redefinition in relation to the nature and purpose of higher education in the national and global context, a period of huge expansion in terms of numbers and institutions and a period characterised by competing agendas of privatisation and affirmative action, with state-funded institutions particularly struggling to keep up with demand (Sabharwal, 2021). This is the higher education context that the massification generation is entering. The massification generation includes a high percentage of students from disadvantaged social groups (SC/OBC/ST: 56%, MoE, 2021). Given the huge disparities in the socio-economic status among students who are entering higher education in the massification generation, there are ongoing equity concerns in terms of students' higher education access and choice, their preparedness for higher education, their participation while at higher education and the outcomes from higher education (in relation to employment) (Sabharwal & Malish, 2016).

One aspect of higher education practice that is common in many contexts but which, at the time of writing, has not been mainstreamed in India is developing a higher education outreach or widening participation culture. Differing from the implementation of constitutionally mandated requirements regarding reservations, a widening participation culture refers to institution-led initiatives, often prompted by national policy frameworks, which aim to open up higher education to previously excluded groups. NEP 2020 includes the aim to promote a widening participation culture for the first time (MHRD, 2020, 14.4.1(g), p. 41), but, at this time, the idea of higher education institutions providing information and guidance to prospective applicants – for instance in the form of open days or higher education fairs – is rare for state-funded institutions. This means that, particularly for massification generation students who have no history of higher levels of education in the family, higher education decisions are being taken in the relative absence of reliable, formal information about courses and institutions (Stewart et al., 2022).

The form of institution where disadvantaged groups are most in evidence is the government college (see Figure 1.1), and students enrolled in government colleges were the participants in the empirical study which underpins this book (see Section 1.6). Government colleges are financially maintained and managed by state governments. These colleges receive funding from the state and charge subsidised fees; these are the institutions where undergraduate courses can be pursued with the lowest financial burden. Government

Figure 1.1 A Government College in Haryana
Source: the research team

colleges are affiliated to a state university and are mandated to follow a particular syllabus set by the university. The syllabus for each course at the university level is regulated significantly by the University Grants Committee (UGC), which is a central government body. These colleges may be co-educational (i.e. mixed gender) (see Figure 1.2), or women's only, and they tend to offer undergraduate courses, though some offer postgraduate courses. There is a huge variation in government colleges in terms of where they are located and the nature of the colleges, ranging from urban colleges which may be highly competitive in terms of both student admissions and staff appointments, to rural colleges which may be undersubscribed and understaffed, with related implications for resourcing. Colleges are also differentiated according to their academic reputation, provision of extracurricular activities, alumni network and reputation for safety. Most government colleges at the time of writing offer three streams of education: BA (Bachelor of Arts), BSc (Bachelor of Sciences), BCom (Bachelor of Commerce), though other qualifications also exist.

Many government colleges serve as local higher education providers to students who either cannot afford or do not wish to stay away from home during their studies. Many students therefore commute to these colleges, with resulting requirements for public transport services. Government colleges may also have lower entry requirements than other institutions. Admission to higher education in India is based on a single percentage mark which is calculated from the Class 12 (end of high school) assessments, though some institutions also hold entrance examinations. While elite institutions require very high Class 12 marks – prestigious colleges in the University of Delhi, for instance, may require 90%; local state-funded government colleges are

Introduction to Gendering the Massification Generation 7

Figure 1.2 A Government College Classroom in Haryana
Source: the research team

more flexible, often accepting students in the unreserved category with Class 12 marks of 65% or 75% (depending on the course). In our study (see Section 1.6), the survey revealed a mean Class 12 mark of 76% for the college in Mahendragarh, 77.1% for the college in Sonipat and 69.3% for the college in Sirsa. Importantly, government colleges tend to be attended by first-generation and relatively marginalised students. Government colleges formed the focus for our study and therefore the empirical underpinnings of this book because, due to the lower fees and dispersed locations, they provide access to higher education for students who often would not otherwise access higher education (Sahu et al., 2017). As such, they are rich sites for exploring gendered higher education access and choice in the massification generation.

1.3 Gender and higher education in India

Research on gender and higher education has long debated the impact of gender on higher education access and choice. However, due to the fact that many higher education systems are now witnessing parity of undergraduate enrolment, the field of gender and higher education research is experiencing a drift away from questions of access, towards other gender issues (David, 2009; Morley & Lugg, 2009). Research that does focus on higher education access and gender often takes a focus on subject choice – particularly in relation to subject areas where women are under-represented, that is STEM – and access to elite higher education institutions, where similarly issues of unequal enrolment persist. Otherwise, the gender focus is often on student experience and participation after enrolment, for instance in terms of women experiencing sexual harassment or discriminatory treatment from teachers and peers and/ or on unequal student success and outcomes. Another focus of research on gender and higher education is to explore inequalities within higher levels of the profession, for instance in relation to the paucity of senior professors and university leaders who are women. All of these areas of research are important in terms of building a holistic picture of gender dynamics and intersecting inequalities in higher education, but arguably there is still scope to research higher education access from a gendered perspective – especially in the domain of higher education *choice*, which reveals inequalities that are masked by a blanket approach to measuring *access*. As such, this book makes an argument for a sustained focus on higher education access and choice.

India reported a Gender Parity Index (GPI) score of 1 for the first time in 2018–2019 (MHRD, 2019), rising to 1.01 in 2019–2020 (MoE, 2020). A GPI of 1 means equal numbers of women and men, and more than 1 signifies that there are more women than men enrolled in higher education. The Gross Enrolment Rate (GER) for women stands at 27.3, which is higher than the GER for men at 26.9, indicating a higher level of participation of women vis-à-vis men in higher education in India (ibid.). The national approach to advancing gender equity in higher education goes beyond the goal of parity of enrolment and places emphasis on non-discrimination, justice and fairness in the distribution and access to resources and opportunities for people to attain their full potential, regardless of demographic, economic, social and geographic status. The approach includes, on the one hand, policies for improving higher education enrolment of women and, on the other, providing strategies to protect women from gender discrimination on campuses. Wider policy agendas have strengthened women's access to higher education, such as the right to free, compulsory primary education and the universalisation of secondary schooling, the laws prohibiting child marriage and the legally supported right to non-discriminatory access to education.

As the concern has shifted away from the parity of enrolment in India, so has the focus moved to a concern with equitable participation and student experience, in particular due to rife sexual harassment on Indian campuses (Sinha, 2019). There have been policy-driven initiatives such as the formulation of regulations for protection against gender-based discrimination and sexual harassment, the constitution of Internal Complaint Committees in higher education institutions, the creation of Women's Cells (where women can go for help/guidance) and the establishment of Women's Studies Centres (for training and knowledge production). Concerns with employment outcomes are also present in the Indian context, particularly where prestigious courses and/or institutions – which are frequented by higher proportions of men students – lead to more favourable employment outcomes; there is a national concern about women's workforce participation, which does not correlate with higher levels of education in a straightforward manner (Sudarshan, 2018). There is widespread recognition that women are under-represented

Introduction to Gendering the Massification Generation 9

in certain courses, such as engineering and management as well as in elite institutions (Chanana, 2007). Research in India has also demonstrated that young women and their families are selecting institutions that may not match young women's abilities, in order to select colleges with a safer commute and/or reputation as a safe college for young women (Borker, 2021). The focus on gendered inequalities in the academic profession can also be found in higher education research on India (e.g. Sabharwal et al., 2020; Sudarshan & Thomas, 2024). Thus, the contours of research on gender and higher education in India follow lines similar to the international research field – here again, specifically in relation to the Indian context, we argue that there is a clear rationale to maintain a focus on higher education access and choice, alongside important concerns pertaining to other aspects of higher education.

One clear argument for maintaining a focus on higher education access and choice, both internationally and within the Indian context, is that there are intersectional differences in higher education trajectories. In the international higher education research field, gender is commonly discussed in relation to other intersecting identity characteristics such as ethnicity (Bhopal, 2008), race (Mirza, 2009) and social class or socio-economic status (Wilkins & Burke, 2013). These studies point out that gender inequalities are rife for underprivileged women. This concern is also strong in the Indian context, where it has been argued that gender parity has been achieved due to high levels of participation of women from *elite* and *urban* backgrounds (John, 2012), with women from marginalised backgrounds facing more challenges (Paik, 2014). Research has shown that women from disadvantaged *social* groups (based on caste, indigeneity, religion) are more likely than other women to also be from *low economic status* groups, are more likely to reside in *rural areas* (Sabharwal, 2015) and are more likely to have studied in *under-resourced government schools* (NSO, 2017). Gendered higher education access and choice are further shaped by religious identities. Scholars have explored how affirmative action policy in India has not addressed the social exclusion and under-representation of Muslims in India (Hasan, 2015).

This book argues that an intersectional approach to analysing gendered higher education access and choice is essential, but we argue in parallel that there are gendered dynamics which span privilege and disadvantage and which shape young people's educational trajectories, even in a context where parity has been achieved. To understand gendered access to higher education in India, it is important to recognise the colonial and post-colonial historical context of women accessing formal education. Access to education in India was traditionally restricted to men from relatively elite or privileged caste and class backgrounds (Naik & Nurullah, 2000). While this is no longer the case, it is recognised that access to higher education for women is often couched in different terms than for men, with women's higher education being associated with them becoming educated companionate wives and mothers to sons who will build the nation (Chakravarti, 2012). Moreover, there has been a plethora of research which highlights how a combination of Indian liberal advocates and reformists such as Savitribai and Jyotirao Phule, Ambedkar, Rabindranath Tagore and Gandhi; colonial motivations and missionary projects worked towards providing greater access to education for women, but within a framing of gender segregation where women are kept apart from studying alongside men (Frykenberg, 2010). As we found in our study, women-only institutions are held up in common parlance as a major force behind the achievement of gender parity of enrolment in higher education, as are distance and online higher education courses which do not necessitate a woman leaving the home to study (Sudarshan, 2018).

The history of access to higher education for women in India traces the persistent presence of patriarchy. Patriarchal norms across India restrict the movement of young women and monitor their movements outside the home (Phadke, 2007). This situation is located within patriarchal and gendered perceptions regarding honour, division of labour, inheritance, dowry and matrimonial practices (Chowdhry, 1995). These motivations influence how families and young women are able to perceive and pursue different educational trajectories and how young men's experiences are shaped by being socialised into becoming primary breadwinners. In short, higher education access and choice need to be understood as situated within wider gendered social norms which point to areas for further study *in spite of* parity having been achieved.

1.4 Analytical approach to gendering the massification generation

This book argues that there is no single 'correct' way of analysing gender in relation to higher education and choice. At the same time, the conceptualisation of gender that we present encourages richer and deeper analysis of gender than is often demonstrated in this research field (Henderson, 2019). Indeed, in research on higher education access and choice, gender analysis is often missing. To reflect – and expose the weaknesses of – this tendency, Chapter 2 of this book deliberately demonstrates a de-gendered analysis of the massification generation. The chapter lays out the scene of social disadvantage, while the remaining chapters imbue the analysis of social disadvantage with a gender lens. The approach to gender analysis that is adopted in Chapter 3 is known as *gender disaggregation*. Gender disaggregation constituted a key step in gender scholarship (see e.g. Elson, 1993). This step is a simple analytical move which exploded many myths of unity and homogeneity within, for instance, impoverished communities. *Disaggregating by gender* simply means separating statistical data into gendered groups, re-analysing and comparing the results for the different groups. Disaggregating by gender has the effect of revealing multiple layers of dis/advantage that are otherwise hidden by homogenising analyses of the whole population. This approach has its flaws, as the process creates its own fixed categories and new forms of homogeneity,

Introduction to Gendering the Massification Generation 11

and is particularly prone to neglecting non-binary gender identities. However, as a form of analysis that exposes the salience of gender, the disaggregating approach is vital as a bridge from de-gendered thinking to understanding how gender is deeply present in higher education access and choice.

The books moves on from a gender disaggregation approach to an analysis of femininities and masculinities, situating the micro-level processes of higher education decision making within the wider social context. Much research on gender and higher education acknowledges gender difference but stops there and does not ask *how* and *why* there is gender difference. This means that gender difference comes to be understood as natural, factual and, in an implicit sense, biologically determined. The scope for transgression and transformation is limited when gender difference is solidified in this way. Therefore, we argue that it is important to unpack the gender norms that influence higher education decision making and lead to the reproduction of disparities, and likewise to locate the transgression of norms and the potential for transformation (Henderson et al., 2024).

Higher education access and choice are steeped in gender norms because there are deeply embedded attachments to what is appropriate for a person of a particular gender, and what is expected of them in the future. Certain decisions about higher education, when examined closely, are explained by or attributed to gendered roles and codes of what is considered appropriate; decisions about young people's education are taken in the context of gendered social norms regarding marriage, work, reputation and honour. It is important to engage in an in-depth exploration of localised gender norms and gender regimes in order to detach gender analysis from biological determinism. This book presents intricate accounts of gender norms in Haryana, India, and at the same time shows how the contextual detail can be distilled and the concepts applied more widely.

The gender analysis approach that is demonstrated in Chapters 4 and 5 is based on recognising the relationality between young women's and young men's lives, given that the society is still principally organised around heterosexual marriage of cis-gendered[3] individuals, the joining of families and property and continuing the family line. Much research on gender and higher education separates women off for analysis without addressing men, and likewise some research does the same with men. We have chosen to craft a chapter on femininities (Chapter 4) and on masculinities (Chapter 5); both chapters discuss how gender norms and transgressions of one gender impact on the other. Expectations and actions of young men feed into and shape young women's futures and vice versa. For instance if the norm is for women to be younger than their husbands, and the age of marriage creeps up for men, this has an implication for the age where women are expected to marry as well. Within these chapters, we also show that femininity and masculinity respectively are most commonly understood as attached to women's and men's bodies but that gendered associations are also attached to clothes, behaviours, certain objects and hobbies, and educational courses – and may also be attached to gendered bodies that do not match with societal expectations. There were no students in our empirical study who identified as trans and non-binary, but we take inspiration from the scarce studies of trans and non-binary higher education access and choice in the international field (e.g. Marine, 2019) and in India (e.g. Mary, 2023; Shah et al., 2015) by keeping our eyes open for gender transgression and resistance to binary norms, even within the most normative of framings.

Chapter 4 focuses on femininities. In brief, the chapter unpicks what it means to say that something occurs to someone *because she is a woman*. Different meanings are attached to the idea of being a woman in different places, and within different groups in a particular context. A vital step in a nuanced gender analysis – and in exploring the potential for social change – is to unpack the abstract, conceptual meanings of femininity in a particular setting. This is because it is these notions of what women are, what they should do and how they should be that underpin common causal statements about the impact of gender – including the influence of gender upon higher education access and choice. Our analysis of femininity seeks to reveal the norms that solidify expectations of what is appropriate for a woman, and how maintaining these norms is both a personal responsibility on the part of a woman and also a shared social process of shaping an individual's gender. Chapter 5 focuses on masculinities and reveals that men are often the silent comparator in studies of gender and higher education, where women are singled out for analysis. Similar to Chapter 4, the chapter unpicks what it means to say that something occurs to someone *because he is a man*. While young women face more obstacles in accessing higher education in India, young men from the massification generation are not free from gender-related restrictions, and it is important to understand the complexity of men's experiences. Our analysis of masculinity involves recognising enhanced freedoms as well as restrictions and pressures that young men experience in relation to higher education access and choice.

1.5 Haryana

The north Indian state of Haryana was the focus of our empirical project. This focus on a single state enabled an in-depth exploration of norms within and variations across one geopolitical unit of higher education provision. At the same time, the book situates Haryana within a comparative frame in relation to other states of India and other national contexts. This section provides a brief introduction to this fascinating state; further complexities and detail are revealed as the chapters progress.

Haryana came into being in 1966 through the Punjab Reorganisation Act 1966. Prior to this, Haryana was a part of Punjab and part of the north-west province during colonial times. This region has a long history of agricultural production, particularly in relation to dairy products, and a parallel history

Introduction to Gendering the Massification Generation 13

of military service and sporting prowess (Chowdhry, 1986), and these trends continue into the present day. Haryana shares state borders with Punjab, Uttar Pradesh, Rajasthan and New Delhi. A relatively large portion of Haryana is included in the National Capital Region (NCR) which demarcates India's capital, Delhi, and surrounding areas. Proximity to the capital has led to parts of Haryana experiencing significant industrial and infrastructural development. In terms of religion, Haryana is largely a Hindu state, with small proportions of Muslims and Sikhs. There are no Scheduled Tribes in Haryana. In terms of caste groups, a slightly higher proportion of the population is SC than the national average, while the OBC percentage in Haryana is almost equal to the national percentage. In Haryana, the 'backward classes' group is divided into two groups, BCA (Backward Classes A) and BCB (Backward Classes B), with BCA availing of more reservations than BCB, with the implication that BCA may be considered more disadvantaged than BCB. The language spoken in Haryana is mostly Hindi, with a Haryanvi dialect occurring across most of the state, and Punjabi being spoken in the area bordering with Punjab. In terms of educational enrolment at primary level, this stands at 104% (meaning that overage children are enrolled), which is almost equivalent to the national average (NSSO, 2022). In relation to the work-force participation rate,[4] for the age group of >15 years, at 42.5% in Haryana (ibid.) this is around 10% lower than the national figure, suggesting that a large number of people in Haryana do not work in the formal sector.

Haryana is a fascinating case for gender analysis. The state has attained high levels of higher education participation for women, but, at the same time, Haryana is often in the limelight for conservative and regressive gender norms, practices and violence against women (Chowdhry, 2011). One of the factors which has drawn attention to Haryana in terms of gender is its sex ratio (Rajeshwari & Singh, 2015). The most recent census (Census, 2011) revealed an overall sex ratio of 877, meaning that, for every 1,000 men in Haryana, there are 877 women. The national average in Census 2011 was 943. Concerningly, the child sex ratio, which is calculated for children below age seven, was even more skewed at 834 girls for every 1,000 boys, compared to a national average of 1,020. This situation is the outcome of regressive gender norms and marriage practices, including dowry and male inheritance, which lead families to perceive daughters as a financial burden and a liability until they are married (Chowdhry, 2004). The disadvantage of having a girl child motivates prenatal determination of sex and sex-selective abortion, infanticide and neglect of girl children (Purewal, 2018). Decades of these practices have culminated in a shortage of young women who are eligible for marriage. The impact of this has been recorded in increasing incidences of trafficking of brides from other states (Larsen & Kaur, 2013). Apart from a low sex ratio, Haryana is also notorious in terms of gender-based discrimination and violence. Gendered concerns and norms regarding honour, inheritance, dowry and caste-based discrimination have led to public debates about the minimum age at which men and women are eligible to be married. These debates are closely associated with regressive discourses regarding honour killings, gendered harassment and assault on women and control over the matrimonial choices of young people (Women against Sexual Violence and State Repression, 2014). In relation to school participation, a higher GER of girls than boys at the primary and secondary levels in Haryana implies that a higher proportion of girls than boys are late entrants to the school system. In terms of work participation rates (WPR), national levels are *two times* higher for men (73.8%) than for women (31.7%); in Haryana, WPR for men is 65.0% which is almost *four times* that of women (17.4%) (NSSO, 2022), which demonstrates the extent to which women are not working (in the formal sector) in Haryana. At the same time, there have been initiatives to change gender norms relating to girls in Haryana, the most notable of which is the '*Beti Bachao, Beti Padhao*' scheme, which spans multiple sectors and activities, including capacity building of professionals and sensitisation of communities (Ministry of WCD, n.d.). Moreover, in recent years, there has been a significant inclusion of women's voices in public spaces and sports. Women from Haryana have been recognised for engaging and excelling in sports and other careers such as law enforcement which are traditionally perceived to be masculine (Oza, 2019).

Haryana does not have a long history of higher education (Mittal, 1986). During British colonial rule, Haryana was positioned as an agricultural area of Punjab, specialising in cattle rearing (ibid.). However, proximity to New Delhi and the planned economic development of the state have resulted in recent rapid development of higher education in the state, including a number of nationally reputed private institutions. According to the Department of Higher Education in Haryana (Government of Haryana, 2023), in the year 2021–2022, there were 424 higher education institutions. In 2020–2021, the GER in Haryana was 31.1, compared with the national average of 27.3 (MoE, 2021). Statistics (ibid.) indicate that more women than men were enrolled in undergraduate, post-graduate and doctoral levels of education in Haryana. Indeed, more young women than young men were even enrolled across SC and OBC communities, with the GPI for SC higher than the national average. From these statistics, Haryana appears to be a progressive state in terms of its higher education provision and enrolment, but there are also other parallel narratives to explore, which unfold through the sections of this book.

As can be seen from this introduction, Haryana represents multiple contradictory phenomena, including recent higher education growth and privatisation, a historic reliance on agriculture, military service and sports prowess, strong rural culture and attachment to the land coupled with economic growth and historically embedded caste-related schisms. Conservative gender norms prevail even while educational levels increase for women. Within this complex and multifaceted culture, how do decisions regarding higher education play out in the trajectories of young people in this state?

1.6 The empirical study

This book is underpinned by an empirical study which was conducted in Haryana in 2018 (Henderson et al., 2021; see Appendix A). The study encompassed three co-educational government colleges in three separate districts of Haryana: Mahendragarh, Sonipat and Sirsa. Across all three colleges, the study included a questionnaire survey of undergraduate students across disciplines and genders (see Appendix B). Across two of the colleges (in Mahendragarh and Sonipat districts), semi-structured interviews were conducted with (i) a nominated member of senior leadership about the background of the college and perceptions of gendered higher education access and (ii) undergraduate students, two women and two men in each sampled college, about the students' biographical trajectories towards higher education, family background and perceptions of gendered higher education access. Focus group discussions (FGDs) were facilitated with five women students and five men students in each college, which focused on perceptions of gendered higher education access. (For more information about the participants, please refer to Appendix B.)

The three districts selected for the study were chosen on the basis of primarily geographical contrast in terms of location within Haryana. Sonipat is located within the NCR and is near to Delhi, with a significant urban population. Mahendragarh is close to the Rajasthan border and is within the NCR but more rural than Sonipat and further from Delhi. Sirsa is close to the Punjab border and is not within the NCR and has a relatively low urban population. As well as being a rural district, Sirsa also has a high percentage of its population belonging to SC groups, as compared to the other two districts and the state average. There is a variation in the presence of higher education institutions in the districts. It is noteworthy that a study of higher education institution concentration in India found that none of the three districts has a 'high concentration' of higher education institutions (Varghese et al., 2018, p. 38).

One co-educational government college was selected in each district based on its location (i.e. not located in the district urban centre) and our team members' connections with the colleges (in order to facilitate access). The colleges were given the following pseudonyms: Mahendragarh District College (MDC), Sonipat District College (SDC) and Sirsa District College (SiDC). None of the colleges offered student accommodation. MDC and SDC offered all three education streams (BA, BCom, BSc), but SiDC offered just two of these (BA and BCom) at the time of data collection. SDC, previously a co-educational college, was in the process of moving over to being a women's college, and the student population in our study was already skewed towards women. At the time of the study, MDC was in the process of opening up more courses to women. However, the college was favoured by men as there was a women's government college in the same urban centre, and women therefore usually selected to study at the women's college. Women wanting to study BSc had to enrol in

MDC as the women's college did not offer that qualification. SiDC was a relatively new college which had been established around ten years, before our study, on land donated by a landowner in the village; the college was located approximately five km from the nearest small urban centre. The college was frequented by students from nearby villages.

1.7 Navigating this book

Gendering the Massification Generation presents a cumulative gender analysis of the massification generation which unfolds across each chapter, illustrated with rich insights from the empirical study.

The first pair of substantive chapters explores the massification generation. Chapter 2, 'The massification generation', sets out the key characteristics of the massification generation, including the educational and employment histories that characterise the generations preceding the massification generation, and how local geographical horizons interact with higher education access and choice for the massification generation students, as well as the schooling histories of the young people reaching higher education in the massification generation. The chapter deliberately avoids a gender analysis. Chapter 3, 'Gendering the massification generation', re-reads the data and commentary from Chapter 2 by exploring gender difference, this time exploring grandmothers and grandfathers rather than grandparents, and mothers and fathers rather than parents and young women and men as opposed to young people in general. Overall, Chapter 3 argues that higher education access and choice are profoundly gendered, against a backdrop of gender parity of enrolment.

The book then moves onto the second pair of substantive chapters, which deepen the gender analysis of the massification generation by focusing on femininity and masculinity. Chapter 4, 'Honour and marriage: femininity and higher education access', addresses key aspects of femininity and how they relate to higher education access and choice. First, the notion of honour is explored, and how higher education decision making is impacted by families' attempts to protect their daughters' honour is seen. Second, the chapter addresses the practice of marriage, and how higher education interacts with marriage and marriageability in different ways. Chapter 5, 'Family responsibility: masculinity and higher education access', covers the dominant masculinity norms. Nuances of masculinity are explored, with specific reference to notions of family responsibility, employability and marriageability, and how these are enmeshed with higher education access and choice. Together, the pair of chapters explore gender norms and gender transgressions and consider how norms of femininity and masculinity need to be understood as intertwined in order to build up a holistic gender analysis of higher education access and choice.

The final chapter charts the journey taken through the book in terms of its presentation of a cumulative analysis of gendered higher education access and

Introduction to Gendering the Massification Generation

choice in the massification generation in India. The chapter also includes considerations for policy strategy and further research and a summary of the gender analysis process presented in the book. Finally, the chapter concludes with a reminder that the questions posed in the book can never be fully resolved and will always need further exploration.

Notes

1 A full exploration of the system can be found in *Re-imagining Indian Higher Education: A Social Ecology of Higher Education Institutions* (Tierney & Sabharwal, 2016).
2 The Constitution of India guarantees 15% reservation of seats for SCs, 7.5% for STs, 27% for OBCs in government and government-aided higher education institutions and 10% reservation for Economically Weaker Sections (EWS) within the general category (i.e. not SC, ST or OBC).
3 Cis-gendered refers to those whose gender identity is aligned with the sex/gender they were ascribed with at birth, that is people who do not identify as transgender, non-binary or other related gender identities.
4 The use of workforce participation rate (WPR), defined as the percentage of total workers to the total population, is problematic in a society where many people are occupied with agricultural work on their own land and/or small business ventures in the informal sector. However, WPR is useful to indicate the differences between men's and women's types of employment (Rajeshwari & Singh, 2015).

References

Ansari, M. M. (2018). Concerns of minority groups in higher education participation: The plight of the Muslim community. In N. V. Varghese, N. S. Sabharwal, & C. M. Malish (Eds.), *India higher education report 2016: Equity* (pp. 201–220). SAGE.

Banerjee, P. (2016). Writing the Adivasi: Some historiographical notes. *The Indian Economic and Social History Review*, *53*(1), 131–153. https://doi.org/10.1177/001946461561954

Bhopal, K. (2008). Shared communities and shared understandings: The experiences of Asian women in a British University. *International Studies in Sociology of Education*, *18*(3–4), 185–197. https://doi.org/10.1080/09620210802492773

Borker, G. (2021). *Safety first: Perceived risk of street harassment and educational choices of women. Policy research working paper no. WPS9731*. World Bank. Retrieved June 26, 2023, from http://documents.worldbank.org/curated/en/723631626710146405/Safety-First-Perceived-Risk-of-Street-Harassment-and-Educational-Choices-of-Women

Borooah, V. K., Sabharwal, N., Diwakar, D. G., Mishra, V. K., & Naik, A. K. (2015). *Caste, discrimination and exclusion in modern India*. SAGE.

Census. (2011). *Population census 2011*. Retrieved September 10, 2023, from www.census2011.co.in

Chakravarti, U. (2012). Rethinking the goals of education: Some thoughts on women's education and women's development. *Contemporary Education Dialogue*, *9*(2), 223–243. https://doi.org/10.1177/097318491200900205

Chanana, K. (2007). Globalisation, higher education and gender: Changing subject choices of Indian women students. *Economic and Political Weekly*, *42*(7), 590–598.

Chowdhry, P. (1986). The advantages of backwardness: Colonial policy and agriculture in Haryana. *The Indian Economic & Social History Review*, *23*(3), 263–288. https://doi.org/10.1177/001946468602300302

Chowdhry, P. (1995). Contesting claims and counter-claims: Questions of the inheritance and sexuality of widows in a colonial state. *Contributions to Indian Sociology*, *29*(1–2), 65–82. https://doi.org/10.1177/0069966795029001005

Chowdhry, P. (2004). Private lives, state intervention: Cases of runaway marriage in rural north India. *Modern Asian Studies*, *38*(1), 55–84. https://doi.org/10.1017/S0026749X04001027

Chowdhry, P. (2011). *Political economy of production and reproduction: Caste, custom and community in North India*. Oxford University Press.

David, M. E. (2009). Diversity, gender and widening participation in global higher education: A feminist perspective. *International Studies in Sociology of Education*, *19*(1), 1–17. https://doi.org/10.1080/09620210903057590

Deshpande, S. (2013). Caste quotas and formal inclusion in Indian higher education. In S. Deshpande & U. Zacharias (Eds.), *Beyond inclusion: The practice of equal access in Indian higher education* (pp. 13–47). Routledge.

Elson, D. (1993). Gender-aware analysis and development economics. *Journal of International Development*, *5*(2), 237–247. https://doi.org/10.1002/jid.3380050214

Frykenberg, R. E. (2010). *Christianity in India: From beginnings to the present*. Oxford University Press.

Ghosh, S. C. (1995). Bentinck, Macaulay and the introduction of English education in India. *History of Education*, *24*(1), 17–24. https://doi.org/10.1080/0046760950240102

Government of Haryana. (2023). *Department of higher education*. Department of Higher Education Haryana. Retrieved June 6, 2023, from www.highereduhry.ac.in

Hasan, Z. (2015). Disparities in access to higher education: Persistent deficit of Muslims. In A. K. Singh (Ed.), *Education and empowerment in India* (pp. 152–165). Routledge India.

Henderson, E. F. (2019). Starting with gender: Definitional politics in international higher education research. In E. F. Henderson & Z. Nicolazzo (Eds.), *Starting with gender in international higher education research: Conceptual debates and methodological considerations* (pp. 12–28). Routledge.

Henderson, E. F., Sabharwal, N. S. S., & Thomas, A. (2024). From gender parity to gender prism: Looking beyond enrolment parity to explore gendered conditions of access to higher education in Haryana, India. In N. V. Varghese & N. S. Sabharwal (Eds.), *India higher education report 2022: Women in higher education* (pp. 19–24). Routledge India.

Henderson, E. F., Thomas, A., Mansuy, J., Sabharwal, N. S. S., Stewart, A., Rathee, S., Yadav, R., & Samanta, N. (2021). *A fair chance for education: Gendered pathways to educational success in Haryana: Phase 1 findings report*. University of Warwick. Retrieved September 10, 2023, from https://wrap.warwick.ac.uk/155467/

John, M. E. (2012). Gender and higher education in the time of reforms. *Contemporary Education Dialogue*, *9*(2), 197–221. https://doi.org/10.1177/097318491200900204

Larsen, M., & Kaur, R. (2013). Signs of change? Sex ratio imbalance and shifting social practices in Northern India. *Economic and Political Weekly*, *48*(35), 45–52.

Leathwood, C., & Read, B. (2009). *Gender and the changing face of higher education: A feminized future*. Open University Press.

Marine, S. B. (2019). Changing the frame: Queering access to higher education for trans* students. In Z. Nicolazzo (Ed.), *What's transgressive about trans* studies in education now?* (pp. 7–23). Routledge.

Mary, S. A. (2023). Structural marginalisation of transgender students in higher education institutions of India. In K. Kikhi & D. R. Gautam (Eds.), *Marginality in India: Perspectives of marginalisation from the Northeast* (pp. 110–126). Routledge India.

Ministry of Education (MoE). (2020). *All India survey of higher education: 2019–20*. Government of India.

Ministry of Education (MoE). (2021). *All India survey of higher education: 2020–2021*. Government of India.

Ministry of Human Resource Development (MHRD). (2019). *All India survey of higher education: 2018–19*. Government of India.

Ministry of Human Resource Development (MHRD). (2020). *National Education Policy (NEP 2020)*. Government of India.

Ministry of Women and Child Development (WCD). (n.d.). *Beti Bachao Beti Padhao: Operational manual*. Government of India. Retrieved September 10, 2023, from https://wcd.nic.in/sites/default/files/Beti%20Bachao%20Beti%20Padhao%20Operational%20Manual.pdf

Mirza, H. S. (2009). *Race, gender and educational desire: Why Black women succeed and fail*. Routledge.

Mittal, S. C. (1986). *Haryana: A historical perspective*. Atlantic Publishers and Distributors.

Morley, L., & Lugg, R. (2009). Mapping meritocracy: Intersecting gender, poverty and higher educational opportunity structures. *Higher Education Policy*, *22*, 37–60. https://doi.org/10.1057/hep.2008.26

Naik, J. P., & Nurullah, S. (2000). *A students' history of education in India: 1800–1973* (6th Rev. ed.). Macmillan India.

National Sample Survey Organisation (NSSO). (2022). *Annual report: Periodic Labour Force Survey (PLFS): 2021–2022*. Ministry of Statistics and Programme Implementation Statistics Office, Government of India.

National Statistical Office (NSO). (2017). *India: Household social consumption on education 2017–2018, 75th round*. Government of India.

Oza, R. (2019). Wrestling women: Caste and neoliberalism in rural Haryana. *Gender, Place & Culture*, *26*(4), 468–488. https://doi.org/10.1080/0966369X.2018.1502162

Paik, S. (2014). *Dalit women's education in modern India: Double discrimination*. Routledge.

Panigrahi, J. (2020). *Fees in private higher education institutions: A study of deemed to be universities in India. CPRHE research paper 13*. Centre for Policy Research in Higher Education (CPRHE), National Institute of Educational Planning and Administration (NIEPA).

Phadke, S. (2007). Dangerous liaisons: Women and men: Risk and reputation in Mumbai. *Economic and Political Weekly*, *42*(17), 1510–1518.

Purewal, N. (2018). Sex selective abortion, neoliberal patriarchy and structural violence in India. *Feminist Review*, *119*(1), 20–38. https://doi.org/10.1057/s41305-018-0122-y

Rajeshwari, & Singh, B. (2015). Status of women in Haryana a spatio-temporal study. *Eastern Geographer*, *21*(1), 503–512.

Sabharwal, N. S. (2015). Looking at Dalit women. In D. Jain & C. P. Sujaya (Eds.), *Indian women revisited* (pp. 61–90). Government of India.

Sabharwal, N. S. (2021). Nature of access to higher education in India: Emerging pattern of social and spatial inequalities in educational opportunities. In M. S. Jaglan & Rajeshwari (Eds.), *Reflections on 21st century human habitats in India: Felicitation volume in honour of professor MH Qureshi* (pp. 345–369). Springer Singapore.

Sabharwal, N. S., Henderson, E. F., & Joseph, R. S. (2020). Hidden social exclusion in Indian academia: Gender, caste and conference participation. *Gender and Education, 32*(1), 27–42. https://doi.org/10.1080/09540253.2019.1685657

Sabharwal, N. S., & Malish, C. M. (2016). *Student diversity and civic learning in higher education in India. CPRHE research paper 3.* Centre for Policy Research in Higher Education (CPRHE), National University of Educational Planning and Administration (NUEPA).

Sahu, B., Jeffery, P., & Nakkeeran, N. (2017). Barriers to higher education: Commonalities and contrasts in the experiences of Hindu and Muslim young women in urban Bengaluru. *Compare: A Journal of Comparative and International Education, 47*(2), 177–191. https://doi.org/10.1080/03057925.2016.1220825

Shah, C., Merchant, R., Mahajan, S., & Nevatia, S. (2015). *No outlaws in the gender galaxy.* Zubaan.

Sinha, M. (2019). Starting with sexual harassment: Gender politics in the contemporary Indian university. In E. F. Henderson & Z. Nicolazzo (Eds.), *Starting with gender in international higher education research: Conceptual debates and methodological considerations* (pp. 179–196). Routledge.

Stewart, A., Henderson, E. F., Sabharwal, N. S., Thomas, A., Samanta, N., & Mansuy, J. (2022). *Supporting gender-sensitive higher education access and choice in Haryana, India: Policy brief.* University of Warwick.

Sudarshan, R. M. (2018). Higher education and gendered norms: Enabling the "use" of women's education. In N. V. Varghese, N. S. Sabharwal, & C. M. Malish (Eds.), *India higher education report 2016: Equity* (pp. 221–242). SAGE.

Sudarshan, R. M., & Thomas, A. (2024). Gendered academic trajectories through research and publication. In N. V. Varghese & N. S. Sabharwal (Eds.), *India higher education report 2022: Women in higher education.* Routledge India.

Tierney, W. G., & Sabharwal, N. S. (2016). *Re-imagining Indian higher education: A social ecology of higher education institutions. CPRHE research paper 4.* Centre for Policy Research in Higher Education (CPRHE), National University of Educational Planning and Administration (NUEPA).

Varghese, N. V. (2015). *Challenges of massification of higher education in India. CPRHE research papers 1.* Centre for Policy Research in Higher Education (CPRHE), National University of Educational Planning and Administration (NUEPA).

Varghese, N. V., Panigrahi, J., & Rohatgi, A. (2018). *Concentration of higher education institutions in India: A regional analysis. CPRHE research paper 11.* Centre for Policy Research in Higher Education (CPRHE), National Institute of Educational Planning and Administration (NIEPA).

Varghese, N. V., Sabharwal, N. S., & Malish, C. M. (2019). *Equity and inclusion in higher education in India, CPRHE research paper 12.* Centre for Policy Research in Higher Education (CPRHE), National Institute of Educational Planning and Administration (NIEPA).

Wilkins, A., & Burke, P. J. (2013). Widening participation in higher education: The role of professional and social class identities and commitments. *British Journal of Sociology of Education, 36*(3), 434–452. https://doi.org/10.1080/01425692.2013.829742

Women Against Sexual Violence and State Repression. (2014). *Speak! The truth is still alive: Land, caste and sexual violence against Dalit girls and women in Haryana.* Women Against Sexual Violence and State Repression.

2 The massification generation

2.1 Introduction

In India, as in many countries of the world where higher education is expanding, a phenomenon is occurring on a grand scale. That is huge numbers of young people are entering into higher education institutions, many of whom come from backgrounds where there is no history of accessing higher education in their families, extended families and indeed the communities in which they live. Many of these young people are growing up in households where their parents and grandparents alike did not attend formal schooling beyond primary or lower secondary school. This means that decisions about higher education, which tend to be heavily influenced by parents and other family members, are often not being taken based on direct experiences of higher education in previous generations. Moreover, generally, these young people are not growing up around family members from previous generations working in what are known as 'graduate jobs', that is types of employment that are marked as requiring at least an undergraduate degree. This means that career planning and consideration of educational pathways are also not based on direct experiences other than those of the present generation. There are other features of this wave of higher education entrants: many of these young people come from families with comparatively lower levels of financial resourcing, meaning that financial considerations enter strongly into decision making about higher education. There is also a tendency for the families and communities to live local lives, with the consequence that accessing higher education may break with long-established geographical patterns of living.

In this book, we characterise these young people as the 'massification generation'. The intention of this term is to situate what can seem to be individual or localised stories in a wider societal, policy-driven move towards widening access to higher education (Bathmaker et al., 2016). It is important to keep both a micro-level analysis of individual lives and a macro-level understanding of the national higher education context in view, as otherwise issues can become individualised or even blamed on localised customs and cultural mindsets. While contextual aspects feature strongly, at the same time it is necessary to recognise that there are common features of the massification generation, which are created by a mass shift in educational expectations from one generation to the next. This shift can even be termed a disconnect, as such vast generational leaps in educational attainment and employment aspirations are rewriting the cultural scripts for young people in India. Not only are expectations changing in the lives of young people, but also the meaning of higher education itself is being negotiated and is shifting as young people from the massification generation – and their families – are trying to make sense of these newfound opportunities for higher levels of education. What higher education is for and what it means to attain a degree and what life as a graduate is supposed to entail – all is at stake for the massification generation.

It is vital to understand the broad characteristics of the massification generation in order to situate the stories that unfold within specific households within the wider narrative of higher education expansion in India. This chapter is dedicated to presenting the massification generation and, in particular, zooms in on those students in Haryana, India, who have accessed undergraduate education from government colleges in small towns and rural locations. As discussed in Chapter 1 (Section 1.2), these institutions are often lower cost and closer to home than other higher education options and as such tend to be selected by young people who are first-generation higher education entrants and who are comparatively disadvantaged. This chapter deliberately skirts around a gender analysis of the massification generation. Often analyses of social disadvantage in relation to higher education access and choice neglect the gendered aspects. By setting out the commonalities of this student population in this chapter *without* a focus on gender, we deliberately replicate common research tendencies, so as to further highlight the salience of gender in subsequent chapters.

The chapter sets out the key characteristics of the massification generation, which are illustrated with empirical data from the Haryana study (see Section 1.6). The chapter moves through the educational and employment histories that characterise the generations preceding the massification generation, situating the present generation in relation to the parents and grandparents who influence their higher education decisions. The chapter then focuses on the massification generation in relation to how local geographical horizons interact with higher education access and choice. A second section discusses the schooling histories of the young people reaching higher education in the present generation.

2.2 Previous generations – education and employment

2.2.1 The salience of previous generations' educational attainment

Exploring previous generations is an important facet of any analysis of higher education access and choice. Decisions about higher education are taken among family members, through their stories and their influences. Indeed, parental permission and support were considered vital for progression to higher education in our study. Even in situations where family members are absent through death or departure, imagined and inherited stories shape a young person's sense of their social standing and cultural heritage (Thomas, 2021). Young people have more or less say in the higher education decisions they take, including having no say at all (as we saw in our study), and the influence of family members from previous generations can be simultaneously strong and relatively uninformed.

In our study, parental support often took the form of encouraging young people to study in order to take up opportunities that had not been available to them (see also Patfield et al., 2021 in relation to the Australian context). Neetu, for example, noted that parents say, 'We did not study, let our children study'. Sachin described that his parents had told him about the poverty they had faced; he was therefore strongly encouraged to make the most of the opportunities, so that he would not struggle in the way they had. This is a hallmark of the 'contingent chooser', that is a young person making higher education choices without deep knowledge about higher education (Ball et al., 2002, p. 337). We found in our project that, in many cases, parents were scraping together disparate understandings of the risks and opportunities of higher education and of different higher education options and resultant career paths (Thomas & Henderson, 2022).

Moreover, parents and family members were making sense of higher education against other post-schooling options such as training courses or moving directly into employment. In socio-economically disadvantaged households, the option of enrolling in higher education may seem risky or even financially impossible due to the necessity of each family member contributing to the household economy (either as a wage earner or contributing to the housework, farm work or family business). Rajvi referred to people she knew who could not attend higher education due to a lack of resources for the commute from villages. She also referred to a classmate who sometimes only attended college once a week as her father said she needed to restrict expenditure on the commute. In addition to the costs, higher education may represent a long period of foregone earnings (wages not earned due to time spent studying, Rice & Egan, 2014), with an unknown end point due to uncertainties about post-graduation employment. In comparison with taking a shorter vocational training course or entering the labour market directly from school, higher education may appear to be a luxury and a gamble:

> People keep their children [working] in their shops in the town. Some think, 'What will be gained with studying [further than Class 12]; we have our forebears' shops and they [offspring] will keep it [the shop] running'.
> (Rahul)

Previous generations make sense of post-schooling options from a position of not having experienced higher levels of formal education and without a clear sense of the purpose of higher education, meaning that higher education choices – for instance directing offspring away from higher education and towards the family business – were being made somewhat in the dark.

A further implication of previous generations not having accessed higher education is that the process of applying to and gaining admission to higher education can be mystifying, with no senior members of the family who 'know the ropes'. Admissions processes are known to be daunting for any student, let alone first-generation students, as they involve multiple administrative steps (Castleman & Page, 2013). In our study, it was clear that many students were struggling with admissions and were trying to enlist the help of other members of the massification generation to understand the process. Sachin said that he and his 'helpers' waited outside the college in a crowd for two or so days to fill the admissions form without managing to complete this step. This was echoed by Amit who went to a computer lab to fill in the form and was given a slip, but then the format was not clear. He was told by the college, 'Go here, go there, come back tomorrow'. Sachin was from a village, and he said there was one internet shop in his village and that there were people there who could help. However, he said that, for homes where no one from the previous generation is literate, they have to hire a graduate from the village for the day to accompany them to take admission, and they have to pay their travel expenses too. It is clear that students without family members who have direct experience of higher levels of formal education are disadvantaged in making sense of higher education admissions processes.

This section of the chapter focuses on the educational backgrounds of the generations preceding the massification generation. In terms of the educational background, we are referring to formal schooling. This does not detract from the rich and multifaceted non-formal educational experiences that should be recognised in any discussions of access to formal schooling. There is no doubt that the generations preceding the students we encountered in the study were highly skilled in many different respects, including agricultural and household skills as well as various trades and home business ventures. We encountered elderly community members during the study whose breadth of expertise was astonishing, and they could not be described as 'uneducated'. However, this book is about higher education access and choice, and there is only one means of progressing through to undergraduate higher education – that is through formal schooling. As a parent, knowing how to navigate formal schooling, including making decisions about type of school and subject choice, and engaging with teachers about students' progress are a set of skills, which is difficult to attain without having passed through the formal education system. Taking decisions that are based on being able to imagine the nature of the education being discussed is completely different to taking decisions based on a vicarious understanding of educational experiences. This is why we prioritise an analysis of formal schooling attainment of previous generations – to garner a sense of the decision-making sphere of the massification generation.

We extend our exploration of multi-generational educational backgrounds to include grandparents. This is not common in research in this field, which tends to focus on the parental generation. We recognise the importance of considering multi-generational experiences, especially in a context where many households comprise grandparents as well as parents.

2.2.2 Having knowledge of previous generations' educational backgrounds

The educational backgrounds of previous generations may form a greater or lesser part of family narratives. In different contexts, stories of leaving school at 14 or not having attended school at all or having been the first in the family to access higher education may have different resonances and may feed into expectations for the present generation in terms of maintaining or enhancing – or rebelling against – family educational attainment. While the specific level of education of previous generations has salience, as discussed further later in the chapter, it is worth stopping briefly first at a consideration of whether there is any knowledge of the educational backgrounds of the previous generations.

For the Haryana study, we included in our questionnaire survey for undergraduate students a set of questions about levels of formal schooling of previous generations, including all four grandparents, both parents and then some spaces for respondents to add other salient family members (recognising that students may not have this family configuration). It is notable that, across the three colleges, there were only valid responses to this part of the survey for around half of respondents. This high degree of missing data shows in itself a lack of clarity about educational histories in the grandparental generation; as Morley and Lussier (2009, p. 72) state in relation to missing educational information, 'the absence of data is data iteslf'. For parents' education, there was a lower prevalence of missing values, presumably because students had more awareness of their parents' education levels than grandparents' levels. Further research is needed to understand students' knowledge of their families' educational histories. However, what we can say of our study at least is that many young people had reached higher education without having clear knowledge of educational levels attained in previous generations (including parents). This raises a question – which must remain a question for now – about the extent to which (lack of) discussion of the educational backgrounds of other family members is a hallmark of the massification generation. If this discussion is *not* a frequent part of family decision-making processes for the massification generation – at least in Haryana, India – then this creates a different narrative for young people's educational trajectories from the narrative where young people have a clear sense of their role in social mobility (breaking new ground) or in the reproduction of privilege (following in the footsteps).

2.2.3 Grandparents' education

We have already recognised the influential role of parents in the higher education choices of young people in the massification generation in Haryana. We can situate the parents in between their parents and offspring in a multi-generational family portrait. It is important not to stop with parents, as the parents were themselves making educational decisions during a period of seismic change in the Indian education system as the country engaged in widespread efforts to open up primary and secondary education. The parental generation was therefore itself engaging in rewriting of cultural scripts relating to the expectations of educational attainment and the wider redesign of life patterns to include formal schooling. By looking across three generations (where possible), we get a sense of the huge social and educational changes that have occurred in a matter of decades in India.

An important first step in understanding the intergenerational shift is examining the extent to which grandparents had accessed *any* formal education. Many students in our survey had no family history of formal education at grandparent level. For students who had recorded the education level attained by at least one grandparent, the *maximum* level of education attained by respondents' sets of grandparents was *zero* formal education for 34% of respondents at MDC, 60% at SDC and 61% at SiDC. Otherwise put, for a substantial proportion of students, there was *no multi-generational history of formal education in the family*. Moreover, a high proportion of grandparents had exited formal education during or at the end of primary level. Only 22 survey respondents indicated that at least one grandparent had attended post-secondary education of some kind[1] (including vocational/technical education for high school graduates); in one case, two grandparents had attended post-secondary education. In four cases, a Master's qualification was mentioned as having been obtained within the grandparents' generation. However, *89.5% of respondents in our study had no multi-generational history of higher education in the family*.

It is vital to keep in view that the massification generation may have broad characteristics, but there are discrepancies *within* these broad alignments. In the Indian society, there is an ever-present reminder of the caste system in discussions of access to higher education (see Section 1.2). Historically, more marginalised caste groups have experienced exclusion from accessing educational opportunities due to the compound effects of lower financial resourcing and social stigma. In our study, *students from more marginalised caste groups were more likely to come from families with no multi-generational history of formal schooling or higher education in the family*. This eventuality feeds into decision making for the present generation, where decisions are, as a result, more likely to be made based on an imagined/vicarious sense of education rather than lived experiences in the parental generation.

2.2.4 Parents' education

As discussed earlier, the parental generation represented a huge shift in the education landscape in India; for parents, there was a much lower prevalence of no access to formal schooling. Formal schooling was, at the time of the parental generation reaching schooling age, part of the expected experiences for childhood. Only 17 survey respondents (5.7%) in our study indicated that neither parent had attained any formal schooling, and 12 of these were attending the rural college (SiDC), where previous generations' access to education was generally lower. The data show a remarkable generational difference. However, it should be borne in mind that at least *some students are making decisions about entering into higher education with no history of formal schooling at all in the immediate family*.

As discussed in relation to grandparents' education, within the already relatively disadvantaged students enrolling in government colleges, there are differences within the student cohort, in particular, pertaining to caste group. Similar to grandparents, incidence of no formal education at parental level occurred in the most marginalised caste group, and the highest incidence of parental access to higher education occurred in the most privileged caste group. In relation to further qualifications, ten parents in the study were recorded as having attained postgraduate qualifications at Master's level. However, *83.3% of our survey respondents were accessing higher education with no parental history of post-schooling education*.

When exploring the potential salience of the formal schooling attained by previous generations for higher education access and choice in the massification generation, it is important to connect the generations as well as examining each generation separately. By connecting the generations, patterns are revealed of linear 'progress' from one generation to the next or of more complex or interrupted generational educational attainment. Our survey permitted us to examine the extent to which the more highly educated parents (in terms of formal schooling) came from families where the grandparents had also attained higher levels of formal schooling within their generation. For students from families where no grandparents had accessed formal schooling, 10.9% of these students had at least one parent who had attained high school, and 5.9% of these students had at least one parent who had post-schooling education. On the other hand, for students from families where at least one grandparent had accessed post-schooling education, for 40% of these students at least one parent had attained high school and for 50% of these students at least one parent had accessed post-schooling education. In the majority of cases (66.5%), the maximum level of schooling in the parental generation was higher than the maximum level of schooling attained in the grandparental generation, though in several cases the level was the same (21.8%) or lower (11.7%). Most often the 'leap' was of around two to four classes, but in a quarter of cases (25.2%), the difference was *ten classes or more*, showing staggering shifts in the parental generation.

For some young people accessing higher education, they were making a huge leap in accessing higher education when their parents had left school in the primary stage; for other young people, their parents had been the ones to make the leap, and higher education was just the next step above the educational attainment of the parental generation. In terms of the horizon of decision making for higher education, the difference between a stepped generational trajectory towards higher education and advancing by ten classes in a single generation represents an incomparable difference in terms of the symbolic significance of higher levels of education within a family.

2.2.5 Employment in the parental generation

A major discussion in higher education research and policy worldwide is the linking of higher education and employability. In globalised neoliberal framings of education, which are underpinned by the logic of human capital theory, a major purpose of higher education is widely considered as developing individuals' human capital in order to stimulate economic growth (Marginson, 2019). The prevalence of this discourse in research and policy alike presents an argument for government funding of higher education, where other arguments such as the benefit to individuals and society of spending time engaging in higher learning do not receive traction. However, the discourse has also been critiqued as deeply flawed, as higher education is for the most part not set up with the inherent purpose of training students with the necessary skills for specific jobs, so in a sense higher education will always fail at adequately preparing graduates for the specific demands of the labour market. Into this conceptual quagmire about the purpose of higher education lands the notion of the 'graduate job' and the extent to which achieving a degree guarantees graduate-level employment. In a massifying higher education system, many young people are opting for higher education courses with the explicit purpose and expectation of gaining a graduate job, in particular where previous generations have toiled in low-skilled occupations and struggled to eke out a living (Wadhwa, 2018). At the same time, in a context where the massifying higher education system is turning out reams of graduates, the labour market becomes flooded with qualified applicants for graduate jobs, which in turn leads to inflated employer requirements and to high rates of unemployment for graduates. The massification generation in India finds itself in this situation (Varghese & Khare, 2021).

A characteristic of the massification generation that follows on from lower levels of formal education of the previous generations is a lack of direct experience of so-called graduate jobs in previous generations. This is particularly salient due to the strong involvement of family members in higher education decision making in India (Thomas & Henderson, 2022). As discussed earlier, not having direct experience of higher levels of formal education means that decisions are based on imagined versions of what higher education entails. Similarly, understanding how graduate-level employment works and the necessary education pathways that lead into graduate jobs requires a great deal of background knowledge of the graduate labour market. It is recognised in the literature that more privileged students and their families engage in long-term planning and strategising from a very young age to prepare young people for graduate professions, while future-oriented planning is less part of more disadvantaged young people's early lives (Reay et al., 2005).

Many young people and their families in our Haryana study were deeply invested in accessing graduate jobs. Among the students, there was a general sense that a degree would boost employability. For example Babli noted that employers 'will prefer someone with a graduation or postgraduation more than a school graduate'; Amit stated that, 'these days, an undergraduate degree has become basic'. This finding reflects a study of labour market changes in two villages in Panipat district, Haryana (Jodhka, 2012). Graduate opportunities were thus desired by the young people accessing higher education through government colleges in Haryana, but they did not necessarily have a full understanding of the higher education-to-employment pathways.

In our survey, the vast majority of students reported on parents' jobs that would not require higher education qualifications. Importantly, we have to take students' reporting of their parents' employment as an approximation, as we know from the qualitative aspects of the study that many parents were engaging in multiple forms of work such as contributing to the family farm, serving in the family business and perhaps a small occasional income stream on the side. However, interpreting the survey results using any conceptualisation of employment, it was clear that the majority of higher education decision making was occurring with no direct experience in the parental generation of the jobs that the higher education qualification was hoped to lead to. The most common employment types for parents included farming, managing or working in a business and working as a labourer. Other jobs included working in education, healthcare, the civil service or the army. From the students' reporting of their parents' occupation we cannot necessarily garner the level of the job, as for instance the students' responses did not capture the rank of their parents' position in healthcare or the army. Suffice it to say that the vast majority of students from the massification generation as captured by our study were not residing in households where there was direct experience of graduate employment, with the exception of older siblings and cousins from the massification generation who were just starting out in their careers.

2.3 The massification generation

Thus far in the chapter, we have argued that the experiences of previous generations – particularly in terms of education and employment – shape the decision-making processes and aspirations of the massification generation through their influences and imagined trajectories for the young people whose lives they are guiding. This phenomenon is also recognised in studies of other states in India, such as Wadhwa's (2018) study of Punjab, the adjacent state to Haryana. This section of the chapter recognises that young people bring their own lives lived to the table when it comes to taking decisions about higher education. Here, we set out further characteristics of the massification generation, zooming in on those attending higher education in government colleges in small towns and rural areas in India. First, we recognise that geographies of scale play an important part in shaping access to higher education. What may seem local for some can appear unattainable for others (Henderson, 2022). Therefore, we explore the local horizons of the massification generation and consider how higher education access and choice may be affected by a highly local scale of living. Second, we explore the schooling histories of the young people in the massification generation. Overall, the section completes the picture of the massification generation in terms of showcasing the key characteristics of young people who are entering into the higher education sector en masse during the expansion of higher education in India.

2.3.1 Local lives and the importance of commutability

Any discussion of geographical factors pertaining to access to higher education must be laid out with clear contextual parameters, as notions of distance are highly subjective (Henderson, 2022). There is a basic geographical consideration for higher education access and choice, which is that higher education institutions are more dispersed than institutions providing lower levels of schooling (Varghese et al., 2018). Generally, there is a higher concentration of primary schools, followed by secondary/high schools and then higher education institutions; this principle applies in Haryana too (Rajeshwari & Karamvir, 2018). This means that each educational decision is made with an expanding radius in terms of what attending an educational institution actually entails, particularly for those who live in villages which only have a primary school within the village (see Figure 2.1 for an example of a Haryana village). An issue arises if the next level of educational provision lies beyond the accustomed spatial horizons of the family members. If, for instance, a family subsists on farming and/or runs their own business, their horizons may consist of the nearest urban centre and neighbouring villages. They may not even frequent the district urban centre, let alone other districts or states. Deciding to attend higher education is therefore not just a symbolic leap in educational attainment from one generation to the next; it is also a spatial leap (Donnelly & Gamsu, 2018).

It has been an aim of Indian educational policy to increase the concentration of higher education institutions across districts in India (Varghese et al., 2018). However, the policy priority in NEP 2020 is to increase provision at *district* level (MHRD, 2020, 10.8, p. 35), while many families operate within a sub-district geographical horizon for the majority of their activities, meaning that

The massification generation 31

Figure 2.1 A Village in Haryana
Source: the research team

even district-level provision is not local enough. Many higher education institutions in India, as elsewhere, provide live-in accommodation for students, known as hostels, and beyond these hostels, there are other accommodation options such as private hostels and staying with relatives. It is an argument we have heard many times in discussions of higher education access in India and beyond – that issues regarding unequal access to higher education would be solved by more provision of hostel accommodation for students from rural areas. However, this argument does not take into consideration the fact that attending an educational institution that necessitates staying outside of the home is simply not acceptable – or even comprehensible – to many families.

The vast majority of the students in our survey (97.2%) were living at home with their parent/s while studying (see Figure 2.2 for an example of a village home in Haryana). Only nine students were not living at home during their studies, with no students who were studying at SiDC, the rural college, living away from home. For those who did not live at home with their parent/s during their studies, three lived with other students, four lived with other relatives and two were married and lived with their in-laws in their marital home. Thus, it can be seen that a feature – even a condition – of attending higher education for this subset of the massification generation is to live at home while studying. This, therefore, necessitates admission at a nearby higher education institution which can be reached within a feasible daily commute.

32 *The massification generation*

Figure 2.2 A Village Home in Haryana
Source: the research team

Closely related to the fact that the majority of the students in the colleges we were studying lived at home during their studies was the fact that the majority of students lived within a relatively small radius of the college. Only 12 students from the entire survey sample did not reside within the same district as their college, with two of these students residing in a different state, but even these 12 students still lived near to the college, just on the other side of the district or state boundary. High proportions of the respondents lived in the urban centre in or near to which each college was located: 35.8% (MDC), 39.6% (SDC), 27.2% (SiDC). Of the three colleges, SiDC was furthest from its closest urban centre, with more students living in other smaller rural centres nearer to the college.

A different measure of locality is time, and we can also explore the local lives of the students according to the time taken to commute to college. Commute time is not a measure of distance, as time taken to walk to a bus stop may be the same as time taken to reach another town in a high-speed train (Ravalet et al., 2015); moreover, journey time is susceptible to inaccuracy, such as rounding up or estimating an average time where a journey may be

The massification generation 33

variable. However, if we add *travel time* to the aforementioned discussion of *distance*, we reach a clearer picture of what counts as a *commutable college*. For all of the three colleges, the mean travel time was less than an hour (30–45 minutes depending on the college). Distance is related to just how difficult it is to get anywhere. Added to distance and time, the *mode of transport* and its availability complete the picture of what commuting to college entails and add to a wider understanding of the geographical horizons of the young people's families. The vast majority of students in our survey did not have access to a personalised form of transport to reach college and as such were combining different modes of travel, mainly walking and taking the bus. Unlike private colleges, the colleges in our study did not provide bus services at the time of writing, but students could access free bus passes for the public bus service, which could be obtained through the college attestation of the student's status. Participants revealed that the buses were often late, or did not come, or some terminated in the middle of the route so they were unable to reach the college. For those with personalised forms of transport, the most common was bicycle. Several young people were using scooters to reach the college. Some students were using rickshaws, including the option of sharing this mode of transport with other students. Only 13 students were dropped off at the college by a family member. It was clear that just getting to college was a huge challenge for many students, even if within the <1-hour commute as noted earlier.

In sum, students attending government colleges in Haryana are living at a local scale, where 'local' is defined as *within districts*, that is the *sub-district* level. While higher education policy tends to consider the distribution of higher education at district level (Varghese et al., 2018), students in our study were living their lives in spatial units within district level. Students were living at home and commuting to college, where commutability comprises *distance* (within c. 70 km of the college in our study), *time* (within one-hour travel time) and *mode of transport* (usually bus and/or walking). This scale of living was common to the families and communities from which these students originated; even this scale pushed at the boundaries of acceptability, as discussed in subsequent chapters. Therefore, considerations of local living should be borne in mind for the massification generation, where the idea of travelling long distances and staying away from home for higher education may not be a common or appealing idea.

2.3.2 Schooling histories

Exploring the previous schooling trajectories of young people in the massification era is important, as previous schooling decisions can be interpreted in different ways. For instance if we have information on whether a young person attended private or state-funded school, we can draw conclusions about family investment in a young person's education, and also potentially about the level of preparedness that a young person may have gained to be ready for degree-level education. This is particularly salient in India and other contexts where the state schooling system is underfunded, and there is a high dependence on the private sector for quality schooling. Parents often consider that private schools offer better quality of teaching and discipline in comparison to state-funded schools, which are known as government schools (Narwana, 2019). Further linked to preparedness is the medium of instruction (MoI). In a context such as India, where there are multiple languages of instruction in schooling (especially in government schools), but where higher education is still predominantly delivered in English, officially at least – and particularly for science subjects – (Borooah & Sabharwal, 2017), knowing a student's MoI from schooling level also serves as an indicator of future choices and challenges in relation to higher education. We already know that young people attending higher education in government colleges often come from families with relatively low levels of formal education, and who therefore are making decisions about their children's education based on vicarious and imagined experiences of higher education. Similar decisions about schooling were also to an extent being taken by students' parents, and this in turn links into the imagined future careers of the students which were also outside of most parents' lived experiences. In this section, we show common characteristics of the schooling histories of the young people in our study and also reveal disparities within this subset of the massification generation.

In India, aside from private and government schools, there are other schooling types such as convent schools. Only four students in our survey had attended other types of school, so our analysis focuses on private versus state provision, across four major periods of education: Classes 1–5 (primary), 6–8 (lower secondary), 9–10 (upper secondary), 11–12 (high school). Enrolment in private schools in Haryana indicates parents' preference for private education, even when households are aware that these schools rely on student fees as a major source of income. The proportion in private schooling increases from primary into lower secondary and then steadily declines into high school. We can only conjecture as to the reason for this, but it is possible that a squeeze on finances with the arrival of younger siblings may cause this, especially because the fees for private schools increase with the level of education or a belief that government high schools are better quality than government secondary schools.

At SDC and MDC, at each level of schooling, at least half of the respondents had attended private school (apart from high school level at SDC: 49.6% private) (see Figure 2.3). In Haryana 48.3% of students (national average of 70.3%) between the age of 6 and 14 were enrolled in government schools between 2018 and 2021 (ASER Centre, 2021). Thus, a larger proportion of students in Haryana (compared with the national average) was enrolled in privately funded schools, a pattern replicated in state level enrolment (NSO, 2017). This level of private school enrolment across all four stages of schooling is unlike the national level, where a larger proportion of students are enrolled in government schools as compared to private schools (ibid.).

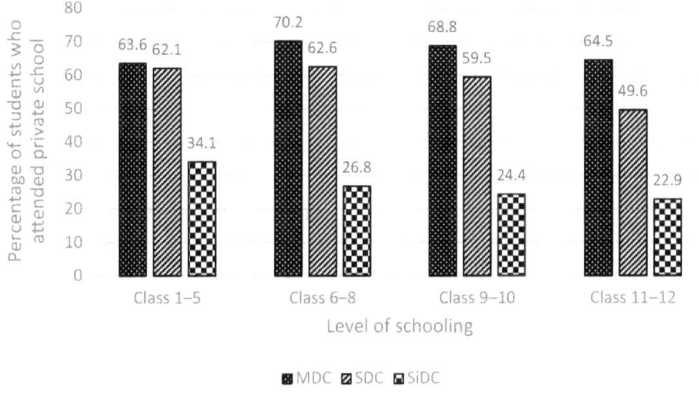

Figure 2.3 Share of Schooling That Is Private by Level of Schooling and College
Source: authors

In contrast to these two colleges, the maximum proportion of students at SiDC who had attended private school was at the primary level, amounting to 34.1%, declining steadily through to high school (see Figure 2.3). Even within a relatively homogenous subset of the massification generation, we can see a stark difference between the two colleges that were located in small urban centres and the rural college.

We can explore the schooling histories in more detail by tracking students' pathways through private and government schooling provision. In our study, we found a higher rate of switching between school type for the more urban colleges (MDC and SDC) than the rural college (SiDC). At SiDC, 64.2% of students[2] started and remained in government schools, 17.3% started and remained in private school and 18.5% switched between provision types at least once. At SDC 38.4% and 22.5% at MDC switched between provision types at least once. This may reflect the more dynamic finances – and priorities – of the students' families at these slightly more urban colleges, in contrast to the rural college where private school was out of the question for the majority of students. Another disparity appears in terms of caste group, where across the board, a higher proportion of students from non-marginalised caste groups had attended private schooling, with the most severe disparities shown for SC students. In terms of switching, this was more common for more marginalised caste groups, perhaps reflecting higher financial instability, except at SiDC, where the vast majority of SC students started and remained in government school throughout.

A final angle of analysis on students' schooling histories pertains to MoI, which is an important aspect of educational trajectories in multilingual societies, as discussed earlier. Not only does MoI at schooling level shape students' ability to succeed in higher education where a particular language is required, but the language of instruction at school may even act as a barrier to selecting particular subjects in higher education – often science subjects. In postcolonial societies which are shaping national education strategies in the wake of colonial influences, often issues of MoI key into deep-set national sentiments about language and national identity (Borooah & Sabharwal, 2017; Rao, 2021). Moreover, these issues may play out differently at different levels of education due to policy shifts and priorities of access. Higher education is more likely to be conducted in the previous colonial language (and/or in English as a 'global' language), and lower levels of schooling are more likely to be conducted in 'local' language/s. This means there may be a linguistic disconnect between schooling and higher education, meaning that those who have already accessed at least some schooling in the language of higher education are more prepared for their entry to higher education. Across our survey sample as a whole, 70.9% of respondents had completed Class 12 in Hindi, in comparison with the national figure for Hindi, 42.1% (NSO, 2017). There were also disparities according to caste group in relation to MoI, which also corresponds with the higher likelihood of attending government schooling among the more marginalised caste groups (Verma, 2014). For instance at SiDC, 100% of SC respondents had been schooled in Class 12 solely in Hindi, as compared with 81.3% of the students from the non-marginalised caste groups. As can be seen from this analysis, exposure to English during schooling was extremely low across the board for our study, meaning that many students would have been experiencing a linguistic disconnect from high school to higher education.

2.4 Conclusion

This first glimpse of the massification generation – specifically young people accessing higher education in government colleges – reveals various characteristics which form the backdrop for higher education decision making. We can see common characteristics, including the majority of young people being of the first generation to access higher education, very little experience of postgraduate education in the family, substantial 'leaps' in educational attainment from the grandparental generation to the young people in our study accessing higher education and lack of direct experiences of graduate-level employment in previous generations. Due to the rapid expansion of higher education in India, there were discrepancies between the parents' and young people's expectations of higher education access. For parents, higher education was an *option among other options*, for example vocational training or direct employment. For young people, higher education appeared for many to be an obvious choice: 'Everyone is studying, so I also should study' (Neetu); 'It is obvious that you have to do college' (Poonam). The significance of the intergenerational shift in educational access cannot be underestimated.

There are disparities even within this relatively homogenous group. Disparities appear along the lines of caste group, caused by historic inequalities in resourcing and social stigma, with young people from more marginalised caste groups making decisions about higher education with fewer direct experiences of higher levels of schooling or higher education within previous generations. Disparities also appear within the scope of students' educational background where, within the broad-brush term of 'first generation to higher education', there are arguably substantial differences between young people whose parents and even grandparents accessed higher levels of formal schooling, and those whose parents left school during the primary stage.

This chapter has taken into consideration not only the experiences of the previous generations but also the lives already lived by the members of the massification generation. First, we saw that those accessing higher education via government colleges in Haryana were living within highly local geographical horizons, often at a within-district level. This reveals that the Indian policy strategy of planning for higher education at district level may not be *local enough*. Students in our study were almost all living at home, and not necessarily only due to lack of affordable or available student accommodation, but also because living away from home to access higher education was in some way unthinkable due to the local spheres of living. This means that *commutability* is an important concept for considerations of higher education access and choice. It combines living near to a college in terms of distance and travel time, factoring in use of public transport (bus) and/or walking as the most common forms of transport. Alongside local horizons, we also explored schooling histories and found that government schooling was relatively prevalent in the more urban colleges and highly prevalent in the rural college. Switching between private and government schools was also relatively common, perhaps due to changes in family fortune or the arrival of other siblings requiring further spreading out of educational investment. A caste group disparity also emerged, with more students from marginalised caste groups having accessed government schooling. This was also discussed in relation to MoI, where more privileged students had studied in English, but still many of the students in our study were arriving at higher education having completed high school in Hindi.

Overall, this chapter has introduced the massification generation as a global phenomenon for massifying higher education sectors and as a national phenomenon in India. The chapter has illustrated this global phenomenon with students attending government colleges in Haryana. It is clear that many of the students in our study have grown up against comparative disadvantage and relatively low financial resourcing. This scene of relatively homogeneous disadvantage sets the stage for the gender analysis to follow, with the exploration of how young people in the same families and communities grow up with different – gendered – options and opportunities for higher education access and choice.

Notes

1 It is important to recall that the respondents for this survey were undergraduate students, many of whom did not have full awareness of their family members' levels or names of qualifications. As such the findings should be taken as an approximation of levels/types of higher education. Qualifications included technical/vocational higher education: JBT (Junior Basic Training – teacher training certificate) and DEd (Diploma of Education). Undergraduate qualifications included BA (Bachelor of Arts), BSc (Bachelor of Science), MBBS (Bachelor of Medicine), BCom (Bachelor of Commerce), BEd (Bachelor of Education). Four postgraduate qualifications were noted, all MA (Master of Arts).
2 Where all four schooling types were recorded and valid.

References

ASER Centre. (2021). *Annual status of education report (rural) 2021*. ASER Centre. Retrieved September 10, 2023, from https://asercentre.org/aser-2021/

Ball, S. J., Reay, D., & David, M. (2002). "Ethnic choosing": Minority ethnic students, social class and higher education choice. *Race Ethnicity and Education*, 5(4), 333–357. https://doi.org/10.1080/1361332022000030879

Bathmaker, A., Ingram, N., Abrahams, J., Hoare, A., Waller, R., & Bradley, H. (2016). *Higher education, social class and social mobility: The degree generation*. Palgrave Macmillan.

Borooah, V. K., & Sabharwal, N. S. (2017). *English as a medium of instruction in Indian education: Inequality of access to educational opportunities. CPRHE research papers 10*. Centre for Policy Research in Higher Education (CPRHE), National University of Educational Planning and Administration (NUEPA).

Castleman, B. L., & Page, L. C. (2013). The not-so-lazy days of summer: Experimental interventions to increase college entry among low-income high school graduates. *New Directions for Youth Development*, 2013(140), 77–97. https://doi.org/10.1002/yd.20079

Donnelly, M., & Gamsu, S. (2018). Regional structures of feeling? A spatially and socially differentiated analysis of UK student Im/mobility. *British Journal of Sociology of Education*, 39(7), 961–981. https://doi.org/10.1080/01425692.2018.1426442

Henderson, H. (2022). *Non-university higher education: Geographies of place, possibility and inequality*. Bloomsbury Publishing.

Jodhka, S. S. (2012). Agrarian changes in the times of (neo-liberal) "crises": Revisiting attached labour in Haryana. *Economic and Political Weekly*, 47(26–27), 5–13.

Marginson, S. (2019). Limitations of human capital theory. *Studies in Higher Education*, 44(2), 287–301. https://doi.org/10.1080/03075079.2017.1359823

Ministry of Human Resource Development (MHRD). (2020). *National Education Policy (NEP 2020)*. Government of India.

Morley, L., & Lussier, K. (2009). Intersecting poverty and participation in higher education in Ghana and Tanzania. *International Studies in Sociology of Education*, 19(2), 71–85. https://doi.org/10.1080/09620210903257158

Narwana, K. (2019). Hierarchies of access in schooling: An exploration of parental school choice in Haryana. *Millennial Asia*, 10(2), 183–203. https://doi.org/10.1177/0976399619853720

National Statistical Office (NSO). (2017). *India: Household social consumption on education 2017–2018, 75th round*. Government of India.
Patfield, S., Gore, J., & Fray, L. (2021). Reframing first-generation entry: How the familial habitus shapes aspirations for higher education among prospective first-generation Students. *Higher Education Research & Development*, *40*(3), 599–612. https://doi.org/10.1080/07294360.2020.1773766
Rajeshwari, & Karamvir. (2018). School education infrastructure in rural Haryana. *The Deccan Geographer*, *56*(1/2), 55–69.
Rao, P. (2021). Teaching and learning English language during the early British Rule in India. In M. Chilton, S. Clark, & Y. Yoshihara (Eds.), *Asian English. Asia-pacific and literature in English* (pp. 43–67). Palgrave Macmillan. https://doi.org/10.1007/978-981-16-3513-7
Ravalet, E., Dubois, Y., & Kaufmann, V. (2015). Territories of High mobility: Micro and macro analysis. In G. Viry & V. Kaufmann (Eds.), *High mobility in Europe: Work and personal life* (pp. 129–152). Palgrave Macmillan.
Reay, D., David, M. E., & Ball, S. J. (2005). *Degrees of choice: Class, race, gender and higher education*. Trentham Books.
Rice, J. K., & Egan, L. (2014). Foregone earnings. In D. J. Brewer & L. O. Picus (Eds.), *Encyclopedia of education economics & finance*. SAGE. https://doi.org/10.4135/9781483346595
Thomas, A. (2021). *The role of families in the gendered educational trajectories of undergraduate students in Haryana, India* [Unpublished PhD dissertation]. University of Warwick.
Thomas, A., & Henderson, E. F. (2022). *A fair chance for education: Gendered pathways to educational success in Haryana. Phase 2 report: The role of families in the gendered educational trajectories of undergraduate students in Haryana, India*. University of Warwick. Retrieved September 10, 2023, from https://wrap.warwick.ac.uk/170400
Varghese, N. V., & Khare, M. (2021). Employment and employability of higher-education graduates: An overview. In *India higher education report 2020: Employment and employability of higher education graduates in India* (pp. 1–21). Routledge India. https://doi.org/10.4324/9781003158349
Varghese, N. V., Panigrahi, J., & Rohatgi, A. (2018). *Concentration of higher education institutions in India: A regional analysis. CPRHE research paper 11*. Centre for Policy Research in Higher Education (CPRHE), National Institute of Educational Planning and Administration (NIEPA).
Verma, S. (2014). Women in higher education in globalised India: The travails of inclusiveness and social equality. *Social Change*, *44*(3), 371–400. https://doi.org/10.1177/0049085714536810
Wadhwa, R. (2018). Unequal origin, unequal treatment, and unequal educational attainment: Does being first generation still a disadvantage in India? *Higher Education*, *76*(2), 279–300.

3 Gendering the massification generation

3.1 Introduction

The massification generation, when considered as a global phenomenon resulting from higher education policy shifts towards increasing higher education access, is characterised by certain commonalities which were set out in Chapter 2. The chapter also discussed disparities within the massification generation, for instance in relation to socio-economic status and caste-based inequalities. However, broadly speaking, we indicated that the young people represented in our study were from relatively similar backgrounds, in comparison with the population at large that includes young people from often very wealthy families studying at elite institutions in India and abroad.

Gender is inextricable from other axes of disadvantage. The remaining chapters of this book are dedicated to showing how a nuanced and detailed gender analysis of higher education access and choice can help us to better understand higher education, no matter how 'equal' higher education seems to be. This chapter builds on the foundation set in Chapter 2 to explore the gender differences which characterise the trajectories and family experiences of young people accessing higher education from the massification generation. We show that *gender is still salient, even when gender parity of undergraduate enrolment has been achieved* and that gender is still significant in contexts where socio-economic disadvantage and other forms of marginalisation strongly dominate the narrative of higher education access and choice. We re-read the analyses presented in Chapter 2 through a gender lens, and thus we can now start to explore *how young women and men from the same relatively disadvantaged families and communities experience higher education access and choice differently because of their gender*. As discussed in Chapter 1 (Section 1.4), this chapter takes a gender disaggregation approach, which entails splitting statistical data into gender groups and comparing the results, in order to reveal inequalities that remain hidden in a de-gendered approach. No students in our study stated any other gender than woman or man, meaning that the analysis in this chapter veers strongly towards a gender binary. However, in a study incorporating participants stating other

DOI: 10.4324/9781003331216-3

gender identities, the process would be the same – to disaggregate by all genders stated.

We adopt the same analytical process, moving through the generations preceding the massification generation, in terms of their education and employment, but this time exploring grand*mothers* and grand*fathers* rather than grand*parents* and *mothers* and *fathers* rather than *parents*. In the second major section of the chapter, we revisit the local lives and schooling histories of this massification generation to explore differences between young women and young men.

3.2 Gendering previous generations – education and employment

3.2.1 *Why a gender analysis of previous generations' education and employment?*

As discussed in Chapter 2, multiple generations of a family are involved in higher education access and choice – even in cases of absence, death and estrangement, due to the stories that remain in place and become woven through young people's post-schooling decisions. Moreover, members of the previous generation/s are often heavily involved in making these decisions, including because many families financially support higher education attendance and/ or bear the brunt of foregone earnings or lost hours of household labour. Having direct experience of higher education or even of higher levels of formal schooling may help parents and other family elders to imagine and understand more clearly what higher education means and what attending higher education involves. Without this direct experience, decisions are made on the basis of more loosely imagined and vicarious experiences of higher education. Having the experience of graduate-level employment in previous generation/s likewise opens up the family imaginary to the opportunities that may be possible for graduates – and how to plan the educational trajectory in order to access these opportunities (Slack et al., 2014). As discussed in the previous chapter, young people from the massification generation may be making higher education decisions without direct experience of higher levels of education or graduate employment within the family, except potentially from other members of the massification generation.

What we did *not* cover in the previous chapter is the fact that, within previous generations of the same families and communities, different family members have different educational attainment levels and different employment experiences. In particular, as we reveal in this section, within families, there are highly gendered patterns of education and employment. Considering that there is some sense of 'following in the footsteps' along gendered lines, and inheriting gendered expectations of lives to be lived, differentiated education and employment in previous generations mean that higher education may be imbued with different meanings for young people of different genders. In this section, we lay out the gendered terrain for higher education access and choice which means that young people of different genders from the same families and communities are positioned differently vis-à-vis higher education. Mirroring Chapter 2, in this section, a gender lens is applied to the previous discussions of, first, having knowledge of previous generations' educational attainment; second, the educational attainment of grandparents; third, parents' educational attainment; and fourth, the employment backgrounds of parents.

3.2.2 Gendering having knowledge of previous generations' educational backgrounds

We have established that knowledge about the educational histories of other members of the family from previous generations is a sign of discussions of education occurring within the family, which then feed into expectations for younger generations. In Chapter 2, we noted that many of the students completing the questionnaire survey for our study seemed to be unaware of the level of education their grandparents had accessed. We noted that valid responses were only available for *around half of respondents*. Here, we introduce two gendered angles: gender of grandparent and gender of parent. We recognise a weakness in our form of disaggregated analysis: it reproduces a normative family model consisting of two heterosexual couples (grandparents) and their offspring constituting a further heterosexual couple (parents), with the student as their offspring. Many families deviate from this model of course, though it is a dominant model in Haryana, India.

Across the colleges, there was a difference in completion rates for our survey between paternal (*dada* – paternal grandfather, *dadi* – paternal grandmother) and maternal grandparents (*nana* – maternal grandfather, *nani* – maternal grandmother) in that there was a much lower completion rate for maternal grandparents than paternal grandparents. This can be reflective of the patrilocal tradition in Haryana for women to leave their natal residence upon marriage to join their husband's family; many students grow up living in close proximity to paternal grandparents. As discussed in Chapter 2, there was a much lower prevalence of missing values for parental education in our survey, and the gendered patterns were less obvious too, although at SiDC, the proportion of missing responses was unequal at 41.7% for mothers and 21.4% for fathers. From the analysis of missing values for grandparents, however, the gender analysis reveals different levels of knowledge of *fathers' parents* and *mothers' parents*, and therefore potentially different values placed on 'following in the footsteps' of paternal and maternal lineages.

3.2.3 Gendering grandparents' education

In many locations of the world, including India, gender parity of undergraduate enrolment has been achieved, and indeed there are even higher numbers of women students than men in several higher education systems. In this sense, gender inequalities in higher education are often portrayed at policy level as being solved. However, what this claim misses is that young people entering higher education during the massification period have gendered family histories of educational access and attainment behind them. These stories do not remain located within the previous generation – as seen earlier, there was knowledge of family educational histories held within the students themselves. Moreover, views about education expressed by previous generations are inevitably imbued with their experiences, aspirations and disappointments. By taking a gender angle on the educational attainment of previous generations, gendered educational histories appear. In Chapter 2, we combined all grandparents to explore maximum levels of educational attainment in previous generations. This approach is common in research in this area, in particular for survey studies: the highest level of education within a household or generation is analysed (e.g. Chakrabarti, 2009). By doing so, this member of the family is constructed as the most salient for predicting or understanding subsequent generations' trajectories. This approach, however, misses the fact that familial educational aspiration or expectation may not easily cross between different genders within the family. There may be expectations of daughters and of sons, and these may not coincide. The reasons for this are explored further in Chapters 4 and 5, but here we unpack the gender differences in previous generations preceding the massification generation, starting with the grandparents.

In Chapter 2, we noted that the *maximum* level of education attained by respondents' sets of grandparents was *zero* formal education for 34% of respondents at MDC, 60% at SDC and 61% at SiDC. This analysis smoothed over the stark gender differences between access to formal education for grandmothers and grandfathers. Figure 3.1 illustrates the educational attainment for grandparents, showing the educational attainment of sets of grandmothers and sets of grandfathers across the three colleges. Breaking the colleges down, the most extreme difference is for MDC, where 73% of sets of grandmothers had not accessed any formal schooling (i.e. neither grandmother), in comparison with 31% of sets of grandfathers. In these scenarios, in the same family, a daughter could be accessing higher education against a backdrop of no multi-generational history of formal schooling among the women of the family, while a son would potentially be accessing schooling with more embedded family expectations and experiences of formal education. There is also gender inequality when we look across maternal and paternal grandparents. In previous generations, and still continuing to an extent in the massification generation, there was an expectation for wives (in heterosexual marriages) to be less educated than their husbands. This therefore means that potentially wives may be coming from families with less experience of education than husbands, in addition to wives also being less educated than their brothers within their birth families.

If we turn our attention to the higher levels of educational attainment, we noted in Chapter 2 that only 22 of our survey respondents indicated that at least one grandparent had attended post-schooling education of some kind.

44 Gendering the massification generation

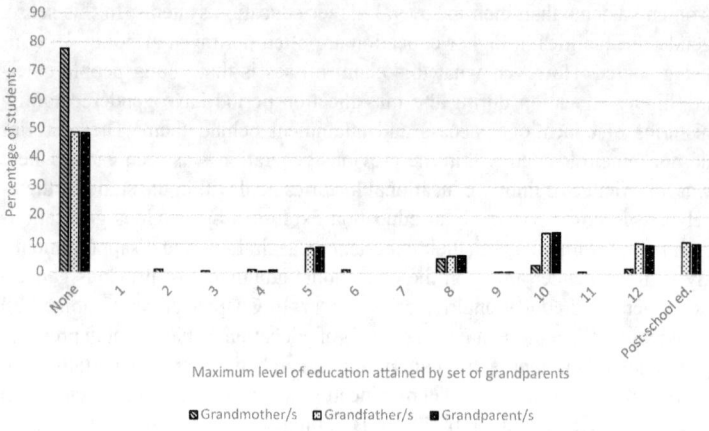

Figure 3.1 Grandparents' Educational Attainment by the Gender of Grandparent, across the Three Sampled Colleges
Source: authors

We can now reveal that all of the grandparents who had accessed post-schooling education were grand*fathers*. This means that no grandmothers had accessed education beyond high school, meaning there was *no multi-generational gender-specific history of accessing post-schooling education for women across our entire study*. Indeed, across our entire sample, only three grandmothers had completed high school, including no grandmothers from SiDC, the rural college. The four Master's qualifications gained in the grandparental generation were therefore also obtained by grand*fathers*. It is clear from our study that the young women and men in Haryana were entering the gates of higher education colleges together but with very different gendered generational histories held within their minds.

3.2.4 Gendering parents' education

As with grandparents, eliding gender difference in parents' educational histories may mask a set of within-family inequalities that are disguised if we track only the maximum educational attainment in the family (see also Bora, 2024). In Chapter 2, we discussed the startling generational shifts from grandparents' experiences of formal schooling to the parental generation, with generational differences even spanning ten classes. These generational differences shift in appearance when we bring in a gender lens and reveal vital intra-family differences that are likely to play out along gendered lines in terms of educational expectations of daughters and sons. Not only are educational expectations affected but also impacted is the potential role that mothers, in situations where they are less educated than their spouses, can play in the educational decision-making within families (Chowdhry, 1999; Thomas, 2021). This section unpacks the different ways in which parental educational attainment is gendered.

In the previous chapter, we noted that, contrary to the grandparents' generation, where lack of access to *any* formal schooling was prevalent, there was a much lower incidence of this in the parents' generation. Only 17 students (5.7%) from our questionnaire survey indicated that neither parent had attained any formal schooling. When we disaggregate maximum education attained for mothers and fathers, a different picture emerges. In our survey, 20 students' fathers (6.8%) had not accessed formal schooling, in comparison with 62 mothers (23.4%). The numbers are both higher than the total of 17 from Chapter 2, as there were cases where the mother had accessed schooling when the father had not or vice versa. It is disturbing to see before us a trend where *the levels of education for women in the parental generation matched or were even lower than men in the grandparental generation.* Within the same families, we can point to *a generation's advantage of young men over young women in terms of histories of educational access.*

If we explore these gendered patterns in relation to caste group, given that there was a higher occurrence of no formal education for marginalised caste groups, we find similar patterns when we compare mothers and fathers. These patterns are particularly pronounced for mothers, as shown in Figure 3.2, where there is a clear stepped trend correlating the lack of formal schooling with historical caste group disadvantage.

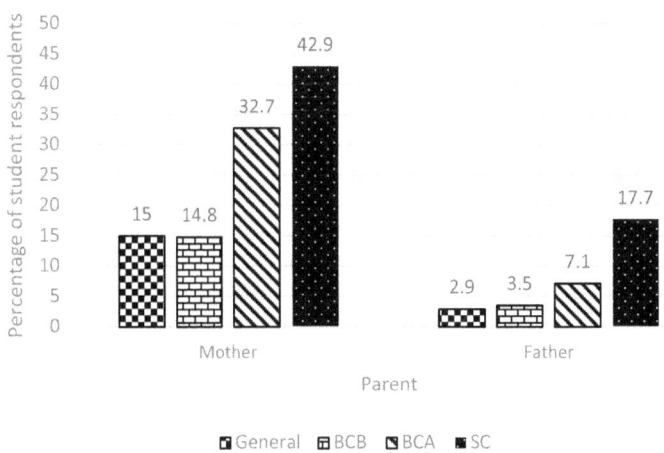

Figure 3.2 Incidence of Zero Formal Education Compared by Mothers and Fathers and Caste Group, across the Three Sampled Colleges

Source: authors

In the grandparents' generation, end of primary (Class 5) was a prominent exit point from formal schooling, but this disappeared in the parental generation, until we disaggregate by gender and this exit point reappears: many mothers exited formal education at the end of primary school. Fathers, on the other hand, were more likely to complete secondary and high school.

This section has already shown the extent to which members of the same families were educated to different levels according to their gender. However, we can deepen this analysis by comparing spousal educational attainment within the same families. In the vast majority of cases, fathers were more educated than mothers. In extreme cases, 13 fathers were 10 levels (classes) more educated than their spouses, with a further three fathers educated 12 levels more and three educated 13 levels more than their spouses. Where mothers had attained higher levels of schooling than their spouses, the difference was in most cases relatively small at just one or a few classes. Where fathers were more educated than mothers, the difference was often larger, at more than five classes. If we return to the analysis of the differences between mothers' and fathers' educational attainment and compare this by caste group, further trends emerge. Students in the non-marginalised caste group were the most likely to have (i) a mother who was more educated than a father and (ii) equal education between mother and father. Parents of students from SC group were least equal, and it is noteworthy that in SC families, only one mother was more educated than the father. This analysis points towards the intersecting nature of inequalities faced by women from the marginalised groups such as those lower in the caste hierarchy (Sabharwal, 2015). In sum, for the majority of pairs of parents across all caste groups, the fathers were more educated than the mothers.

The final analysis we present here pertains to gender differences in access to post-schooling education in previous generations. This has considerable importance for the wider arguments about the gendered generational experiences of the massification generation being presented in this book. In general, being 'first generation' is not explored from a within-family gendered perspective. We argue that it is vital to explore the status of 'first generation' as a gendered phenomenon, where for instance daughters may be the first generation *of women* in a family to access education beyond high school. In Chapter 2, we reported that, for 50 survey respondents across the three colleges (16.7%), at least one parent had attended some form of post-schooling education. If we disaggregate post-schooling education in the parental generation by gender, differences open up. Across the three colleges, 15 students' mothers (5.7%) had gained post-schooling qualifications (none at SiDC). The figure for fathers is almost threefold, at 43 (14.6%, including three at SiDC). From this analysis, we can see that *more sons were approaching higher education decision making with their fathers' direct experience in their minds, than daughters were contemplating higher education with direct post-schooling educational experiences of their mothers behind them.*

Gendering the massification generation 47

Haryana is known to be a highly patriarchal society (see Section 1.5), and these inequalities reflect the cultural dynamics of the context. From our study we can see that, in the majority of families, mothers and fathers did not have an equal footing in terms of their own direct experiences of education. This must have combined with other gender dynamics (discussed further in Chapters 4 and 5) to create unequal power and voice in the family decision-making processes about the education of the next generation (Gautam, 2015). Moreover, differently gendered educational experiences of previous generations surely lead to some gendered expectations and aspirations for the next generation. It is clear from our analysis that, in many cases, there was approximately a whole generation of 'progress' in terms of access to formal schooling separating daughters and sons. This meant that *many daughters were making significant leaps in their educational attainment*, where *many sons simply represented the next increment in terms of generational educational upward mobility*. Different parts of India and different country contexts may reveal different trends within families, depending on gendered interpretations of education and differential expectations of daughters and sons within the same families. We do not claim that the patterns shown in this section reflect a universal pattern. What we show here is the necessity of exploring gender differences within the same family group in order to understand the educational values and histories that accompany any young person on their schooling journeys and as they contemplate accessing higher education.

3.2.5 Gendering employment in the parental generation

The important association of higher education with employment prospects was discussed in Chapter 2, in particular the challenges that massification generation students face where their parents neither attended higher education nor experienced so-called 'graduate jobs'. In Chapter 2, we discussed that many of the students in our study were aspiring for graduate jobs, for example in education, finance and the military. The aspiration for graduate-level employment was evident across genders. The gendered angle of this section emerges when we disaggregate parents' employment by gender, which reveals a *highly gendered pattern of parental employment, irrespective of parental educational attainment*. Often in analyses of employment background, the highest level of job in the family is considered, without acknowledging that this job tends to be held by a man within the family. As with educational aspirations, we argue that there may be gender-specific expectations and hopes for sons' and daughters' post-education lives which mean that a father with a graduate-level job may not lead to a daughter aspiring for the same, if a generational norm of women's workforce participation has not been set.

Importantly, we are not arguing that formal employment is the only purpose of higher education. However, in a world where workforce participation is associated with personal and national economic growth – and therefore power – the fact that women in India have a low workforce participation rate signals potential disempowerment of women in the household economy. This is a national phenomenon in India, and many scholars are charting declines in workforce participation for women, even as their participation in higher education is increasing (Sudarshan, 2018). As discussed in Chapter 1 (Section 1.5), Haryana has a particularly low women's workforce participation rate. This phenomenon leads into further discussions later in the book about the gendered meanings and purposes of higher education for daughters and sons. An important point to make here, however, is that the vast majority of young men in our study were entering into higher education with the lived experiences of workforce participation of their fathers, while the vast majority of young women in our study saw their mothers working in the home.

In our study, almost all of the survey respondents recorded that their mothers were homemakers (92%). As discussed in Chapter 2, it is highly possible that mothers were also working on the land and in family businesses and engaging in small informal revenue-gaining ventures (e.g. caring for buffalo and making and selling *gobar ke uple* or dung fuel cakes) alongside managing the household (Chowdhry, 1993). However, we can only reiterate the fact that their offspring recorded homemaker as the primary employment. Only 13 students' mothers were recorded as having other jobs across the entire survey sample. The other jobs recorded for mothers were teaching, business, government job, professional childcare, farming, skilled/technical labour and nursing. No students reported that their fathers were homemakers. The majority of fathers of students in the survey sample were employed in farming, business or labour. These proportions are to be expected in small urban centres within an agricultural state. Other designations included skilled/technical labour, government job, private job, armed forces, education, priest.

We explored our data from the interviews and FGDs with students to see if further information emerged about mothers' employment or occupations. While several participants told short narratives about their fathers' employment history in among other discussions, only one participant, Sachin, mentioned his mother, who was a homemaker. Students told short narratives about their fathers' employment history. For instance, Rajvi's father managed a family shop – she recounted that he had previously occupied a government position, but at that time salaries were low and irregular, and he had left his job in order to manage his own business. There was a caste-related angle to fathers' employment, in that farming and business were dominated by more privileged groups, and a higher proportion of fathers from more marginalised groups were labourers (Jodhka, 2012). While the majority of students' fathers were not working in graduate jobs, disparities are revealed when we see that the students from more privileged groups had seen their fathers running their own business or farm, while students from more marginalised groups had seen their fathers being given orders from those owning the businesses and farms (Chowdhry, 1993).

Gendering the massification generation 49

Zooming back out to the massification generation, as represented in our study of students enrolled in government colleges in Haryana, it becomes clear that parental employment is highly gendered. Graduate-level employment was scarce in the parental generation. Formal employment was almost non-existent among mothers, meaning that young women aspiring to gain graduate jobs or even jobs of any kind after completing higher education for the most part had no direct family history of women's employment to call on as a precedent. For young men, on the other hand, their aspirations for graduate jobs – and their families' aspirations for them – had more of a foundation in the employment histories of their fathers.

3.3 Gendering the massification generation

Young people growing up in the massification generation in India and beyond are surrounded by gendered histories of family members, including differential education and employment patterns within the family. Young men are more likely to have a history of higher educational attainment and of employment behind them in their fathers and grandfathers than women in their mothers and grandmothers. Alongside these within-family differences, there are also differences in the lives that these young people have already led before reaching higher education, and which are intertwined with the family histories and aspirations. In Chapter 2, we discussed the massification generation in terms of local horizons and schooling histories. Here, we revisit both of these aspects of the massification generation but delve into the differences that we found between young men and women growing up in the same families and communities, meaning that their experiences of accessing higher education were shaped differently along gendered lines.

In discussing gender differences within the massification generation, an important aspect arises – that of sibling order. In Chapter 2 (Section 2.4), we noted that the presence of siblings is important for nuanced analyses of 'first generation' students to higher education. This is because children who are born later may be able to follow in the footsteps of their older siblings in applying for higher education. There are therefore differences within the same family in terms of the presence of direct experience of higher education, which can assist other members of the family to access higher education. This section focuses on the important differences which emerge when we bring gender into the picture. Haryana, as with many parts of India and elsewhere, is a society that is dominated by *son preference*, that is families hoping to give birth to boy children (Mitra, 2014). Son preference results in practices which include *trying for a son*, where families continue to have children until they have a boy child, as well as sex-selective abortion and the neglect, premature weaning and even infanticide of baby girls (Chowdhry, 1999; John et al., 2008). The sibling structure of many of the students' families in our study showed an imbalance resulting from trying for a son, characterised by more older sisters and more younger brothers. This meant that young women in the massification generation, as older sisters, were more likely to be navigating higher levels of education before their brothers. In spite of having lower levels of educational attainment among previous generations of women in the family, it was often the young women who were having to learn about and navigate high school and higher education before their brothers.

We introduce considerations of the impact of son preference on gendered differences in higher education access for young men and women in the massification generation in this chapter and go on to explore the nuances which relate to inheritance and land (see Section 1.5) in more detail in Chapters 4 and 5.

3.3.1 Gendering local lives and the importance of commutability

In Chapter 2, we established that a feature of the massification generation communities represented within our study was a local horizon in terms of spatial mobility. Through the interviews and FGDs, as well as informal exchanges, we became aware of situations where some siblings (more often sisters) were attending their local college, and other siblings (more often brothers) had enrolled in higher education further afield. Our study captures that, in the communities attending government colleges in Haryana, living local lives and choosing local higher education were features of young men's and young women's higher education. Even while the gender differences were less pronounced in this regard than in other aspects analysed in this chapter, nuances still emerged. For instance of those few respondents who were not living at home with parent/s during their studies, two were married women living in their *sasural* (marital home, i.e. with in-laws). Given that it is a common practice in Haryana for women to relocate to their husbands' home upon marriage (Chowdhry, 1997), this is a specifically gendered feature of married women's access to higher education. We explore this glimpse of the role of marriage in HE access and choice further in Chapters 4 and 5.

In terms of living local lives, a major gender issue emerges when we explore the spatial mobility of young women, as opposed to that of young men. The underpinnings of women's restricted mobility are explored in depth in the next chapter, but again some basic differences can be charted in relation to local lives just by disaggregating the analysis presented in Chapter 2. For both MDC and SDC, men students in our survey reported a longer average commute than the women students. At SiDC, the mean commute was almost the same for young women and young men. While the differences are not stark, there is some sense that perhaps the young women in the study were studying at the closest college to home, while – particularly with MDC, which had a good academic reputation – young men may have chosen to attend a college that was further from home. At SiDC, there was no other choice of college in the vicinity.

Some subtle differences also appear when we disaggregate the mode of transport that young people used to reach college, noting that local lives are also shaped by access to different modes of transport. The analysis represents the popularity of the different options (i.e. the proportion of respondents having selected the option in question). It emerged from our disaggregated analysis that, for women students at MDC and SDC, walking was the most common mode of transport, and bus came second. For men students at these colleges, the bus was the most common mode, and walking was the second most common mode. At SiDC, given the rurality of the college, the most common mode for both young women and men was the bus. All three respondents who used the train to reach their college were men. In Chapter 2, we referred to general problems with bus travel for all commuting students, such as the unreliability of services. The prevalence of walking for women students and lower bus use can be related to specific gendered concerns about women's use of public transport (Borker, 2021; Safetipin, 2018). These issues are explored in more depth in Chapter 4, but to gain an initial understanding here, we can refer to a discussion about bus travel among women students in the FGD at MDC, where the students stated that buses were a masculine-dominated space, where there are few women and many men, and that when women take the bus 'there are a lot of problems, boys say a lot of things'. The students went on to explain that, in some cases where bus travel is the only option for accessing a college, *families' reluctance for their daughters to travel in buses prevents these young women from accessing higher education.*

When we explore gendered differences in mode of transport, questions open up about travel time and distance. For instance, at MDC, the mean travel time for the commute to college was 15 minutes longer for men students than women, and women were more likely than men to include walking in their commute. This means that potentially the men students could be travelling much greater distances than women by using the bus and spend an extra 15 minutes of travel time. These subtle differences start to develop a picture where, even for these young people, all of whom were attending nearby colleges, the radius of college choice may be even smaller for young women than for men.

3.3.2 Gendering schooling histories

When exploring schooling histories in Chapter 2, it became clear that, even within the subset of the massification generation that we have explored in our study, there were disparities between schooling histories of young people from different caste groups and between those studying at the rural versus the urban colleges. Students from less privileged groups were seen to have accessed schooling through the government route, which in India is a relatively impoverished system, and/or switched between private and government schooling, reflecting changing family circumstances or investment decisions. We noted that the majority of the students completing our survey had received their schooling in Hindi. In this section, we reveal discrepancies between schooling choices for young men and women from the same families and communities.

School-type choices represent family decisions about educational investment. Since private schooling represents a significant financial investment over a sustained period, parents and/or other relatives funding this have to believe in paying for the education of the child in question. As we have already seen in Chapter 2, within the same communities, there were young people attending both schooling types and indeed switching between types. As such, the young people must have had a sense of the meaning – and the value – placed upon each schooling type, and equally they must have sensed the differentiated value of those whose private schooling was prioritised. It is well known that, in contexts where private schooling occupies a large portion of the market, where the state system is weakened and where families are struggling to make ends meet, that investment in private education is most often channelled towards sons (Narwana, 2019).

In our study, *a higher proportion of young men than young women had been educated privately, across all four levels of schooling* (see Figure 3.3). Moreover, the *gap widened as the level of schooling increased*. In primary school, the difference was negligible but widened significantly up to high school. What we seem to be seeing in our data is an increase in the inequality of schooling type as time goes on, potentially meaning that young women are being *transferred out of private schooling as their educational level increases*. We can conjecture that this may reflect the arrival of younger siblings, including younger brothers, as parents engaged in the son preference-related practice of 'trying for a son', which would have then placed more pressure on the family finances.

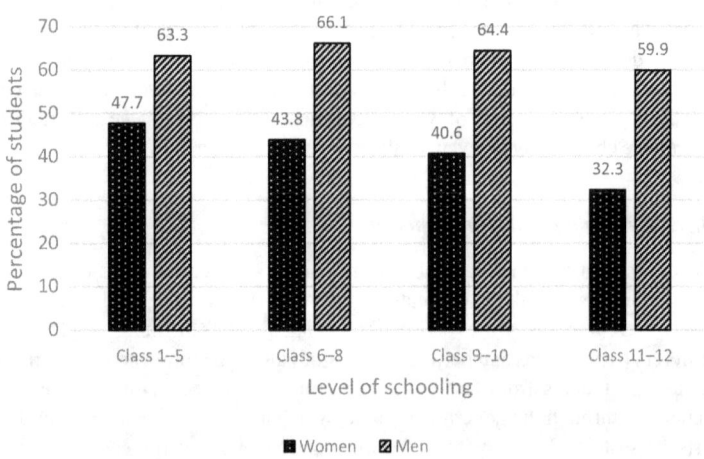

Figure 3.3 Proportion of Students Who Attended Private School by Level of Education and Gender, across All Three Sampled Colleges

Source: authors

These discrepancies become even clearer when we examine schooling pathways in more detail. If we take the two more urban colleges (MDC and SDC) together, switching between private and government education appeared as a gendered phenomenon, where 38.6% of young women had switched school type at least once versus 23.9% of young men. Exploring the pathway where young people begin in private education and stay there for all four levels, 54.5% of young men had experienced this stability in educational investment, in comparison with 37.5% of young women. At the rural college, 94.7% of young women had started and remained in government school for all four levels, compared with 34.1% of young men. Switching pathways was less common for women in the rural college; only 5.3% of young women had switched at least once, as compared with 31.7% of young men. At SiDC, *none of the young women had started and remained in private school*, as compared with 34.1% of men students. It is important to point out that the urban colleges and rural college revealed two different gendered patterns (women switching school type in MDC and SDC and men switching in SiDC), but, in both cases, the young men students were privileged in terms of the family investment, reflecting son preference norms. This finding was corroborated by Kamna, who referred to the fact that, 'if there is a financial problem, they [families] will first choose boys to support further'.

Finally, even in a situation where the majority of students had been schooled in Hindi (in high school), gender differences open up when we disaggregate the data. As we have seen, in a society such as India where postcolonial relations and globalisation priorities privilege English as the preferred MoI, being schooled in English is a marker of prestige. In our survey, 16.1% of young men had been schooled in English in high school versus 10.2% of young women. Inequalities open further when we explore those who were schooled in Classes 11 and 12 uniquely in Hindi, where 63.2% of young men had been schooled in Hindi versus 78.1% of young women.

3.4 Conclusion

Chapter 2 provided a first glimpse of the massification generation and, in particular, revealed both commonalities and disparities within a subset of the massification generation – the young people accessing higher education in government colleges in Haryana, India. Chapter 3 layered this portrait of a generation with a gender disaggregation analysis. By doing so, the chapter revealed that a relatively homogenous-appearing set of young people, all of whom had accessed higher education in the same colleges, was in fact riven with gender differences – and, in many cases, gender disparities. The chapter overall argued that, when we explore higher education access and choice without conducting a gender analysis, we may miss fundamental gender differences playing out within the same families and communities. Second, the chapter argued that, beneath access to higher education as a measure of educational success, young people are arriving at higher education with different expectations placed on them and different experiences behind them. Even where gender parity of enrolment has been achieved and indeed surpassed, this does not mean that the equality of expectation and experience has been achieved. We found in our study that the young women in our study had been disadvantaged *compared to their brothers* across each aspect of our analysis.

In re-reading the analysis of previous generations presented in Chapter 2, we found that the knowledge of maternal grandparents' education was lower than of the paternal side; that, even among generally lower educational attainment in the grandparental generation, grandmothers were more likely to have received little or no formal schooling than grandfathers; that, even among low rates of higher education access across the board, no grandmothers had accessed higher education at all, and very few had completed high school; that, in the parental generation, *mothers'* educational attainment to an extent matched *grandfathers'* schooling histories, meaning they were at times a generation 'behind' their husbands in terms of access to schooling; that mothers had exited formal schooling at earlier points than fathers; that many mothers had a vastly lower educational attainment than their spouses; that almost all mothers were working in the home, irrespective of education, while no fathers were working in the home, and there was a universal expectation of men's participation in the labour market.

We also re-read the analysis of the young people of the massification generation that was presented in Chapter 2. This was against the backdrop of son preference, where young men are the preferred offspring, which leads to an imbalance of older sisters and younger brothers in the sibling order, and older sisters are obliged to navigate higher levels of schooling and higher education before their brothers. Son preference also leads to differential investment in sons and daughters. We found that, even though all young people were living local lives, differential access to forms of transport – particularly related to the risk associated with bus travel for women – potentially meant that young women's lives were even more local than young men's lives. Moreover, we found that choice of school type reflected son preference according to the family means: in the more urban colleges, sons had a higher likelihood of private school education, while daughters seemed to be switching between private and government schools according to families' investment means and/or priorities; in the rural college, daughters were confined to state schooling, while sons reflected pathway switching tendencies, presumably in accordance with these poorer families' shifting financial means. Sons also had more access to English MoI, while more daughters were more often educated in Hindi.

This set of findings produces a different trajectory for daughters and sons from the same families and communities. For daughters, by accessing higher education, they were often making a huge generational leap in terms of formal schooling, meaning their actions were somewhat radical and breaking boundaries. In our study, we also found that young women's higher education was unfolding against the backdrop of the homemaker traditions of previous generations. Young women were living even more localised lives than their brothers in these communities, often walking or travelling by bus but with risk attached. Young women watched their brothers attend private schools, while they themselves were moved between schools according to the family fortunes or arrival of new siblings. Alternatively, young women were attending government schools while they watched their families striving to find finances to send their brothers to private schools, at least temporarily. Finally, young women were watching their brothers gain more access to English, potentially entering into higher education with linguistic abilities different than the siblings with whom they had grown up.

For young men, by accessing higher education, they were often taking the logical next step in a stepped sequence of increased educational attainment through generations. Moreover, their plans to enter the graduate labour market were again just a reflection of the expectation placed upon them to participate in the labour market, with the additional layer of their higher-level qualification. Young men were living local lives but seemed to have more access to more means of transport and therefore wider geographical areas, with fewer risks attached to bus travel. Young men were watching their sisters switch between schooling types, while they remained in private education, or they watched their families struggle to finance their own private schooling even as their sisters were permanently placed in government schools. Young men were accessing more English-medium education than their sisters and entering into higher education more prepared to learn in English.

From sketching out these two trajectories, we can see that higher education access and choice were entered into very differently by young women and men from the same – relatively disadvantaged – families and communities in Haryana, India. The techniques and angles of gender analysis presented in this chapter are applicable beyond Haryana, and beyond India; even though the exact patterns and tendencies are contextually specific, there are many ways in which research on the massification generation across international contexts could benefit from engaging in more gender disaggregation analysis such as that presented in this chapter. However, many questions remain. This chapter has painted a picture of gender difference as a fact, but it is important to unpack the 'factual', often naturalised understanding of gender difference, to understand the norms that lead to the reproduction of difference and disparity and simultaneously to locate transgression and the potential for transformation existing alongside these norms. This is the work of the next two chapters.

References

Bora, M. (2024). Gender, inter-generational mobility and higher education. In N. V. Varghese & N. S. Sabharwal (Eds.), *India higher education report 2022: Women in higher education* (pp. 119–143). Routledge India.

Borker, G. (2021). *Safety first: Perceived risk of street harassment and educational choices of women. Policy research working paper no. WPS9731*. World Bank. Retrieved June 26, 2023, from http://documents.worldbank.org/curated/en/723631626710146405/Safety-First-Perceived-Risk-of-Street-Harassment-and-Educational-Choices-of-Women

Chakrabarti, A. (2009). Determinants of participation in higher education and choice of disciplines: Evidence from urban and rural Indian Youth. *South Asia Economic Journal, 10*(2), 371–402.

Chowdhry, P. (1993). High participation, low evaluation: Women and work in rural Haryana. *Economic and Political Weekly, 28*(52), A135–A148.

Chowdhry, P. (1997). A matter of two shares: A daughter's claim to patrilineal property in rural North India. *The Indian Economic and Social History Review, 34*(3), 289–320. https://doi.org/10.1177/001946469703400

Chowdhry, P. (1999). Ideology, culture and hierarchy: Expenditure-consumption patterns in rural households. In K. Sangari & U. Chakravarti (Eds.), *From myths to markets: Essays on gender* (pp. 274–311). Manohar Publishers and Distributors.

Gautam, M. (2015). Gender, subject choice and higher education in India: Exploring "choices" and "constraints" of women students. *Contemporary Education Dialogue, 12*(1), 31–58. https://doi.org/10.1177/0973184914556865

Jodhka, S. S. (2012). Agrarian changes in the times of (Neo-liberal) "crises": Revisiting attached labour in Haryana. *Economic and Political Weekly, 47*(26–27), 5–13.

John, M. E., Kaur, R., Palriwala, R., Raju, S., & Sagar, A. (2008). *Planning families, planning gender: The adverse child sex ratio in selected districts of Madhya Pradesh, Rajasthan, Himachal Pradesh, Haryana and Punjab*. ActionAid.

Mitra, A. (2014). Son preference in India: Implications for gender development. *Journal of Economic Issues, 48*(4), 1021–1037. https://doi.org/10.2753/JEI0021-3624480408

Narwana, K. (2019). Hierarchies of access in schooling: An exploration of parental school choice in Haryana. *Millennial Asia, 10*(2), 183–203. https://doi.org/10.1177/0976399619853720

Sabharwal, N. S. (2015). Looking at Dalit women. In D. Jain & C. P. Sujaya (Eds.), *Indian women revisited* (pp. 61–90). Government of India.

Safetipin. (2018). *A rapid study on women's safety in public spaces in Rohtak, Haryana*. Safetipin. Retrieved June 30, 2023, from https://safetipin.com/report/a-rapid-study-on-womens-safety-in-public-spaces/

Slack, K., Mangan, J., Hughes, A., & Davies, P. (2014). "Hot", "Cold" and "Warm" information and higher education decision-making. *British Journal of Sociology of Education, 35*(2), 204–223. https://doi.org/10.1080/01425692.2012.741803

Sudarshan, R. M. (2018). Higher education and gendered norms: Enabling the "Use" of women's education. In N. V. Varghese, N. S. Sabharwal, & C. M. Malish (Eds.), *India higher education report 2016: Equity* (pp. 221–242). SAGE.

Thomas, A. (2021). *The role of families in the gendered educational trajectories of undergraduate students in Haryana, India* [Unpublished PhD dissertation]. University of Warwick.

4 Honour and marriage
Femininity and higher education access

4.1 Introduction

So far, this book has established that young people of different genders enter into the decision-making process about attending higher education from different positions, based on gendered family histories of education and employment and gendered expectations and aspirations which are placed on young people as they enter the post-schooling phase of their lives. Chapter 3 showed that young women growing up in Haryana, India, are located in intergenerational trajectories of women in their families, where higher education signifies an unprecedented step; we also showed that, for young men growing up in the same families and communities, the meaning of higher education was more straightforward in terms of an intergenerational march towards upward social mobility. These glimpses of differentiated expectations for young men and young women, of differentiated meanings of higher education, require in-depth unpacking in order to reach a more replete understanding of how higher education access and choice are gendered.

This chapter unpacks the gendered norms – and the potential for transgression and resistance – for young women accessing higher education in government colleges in Haryana, India. Dominant codes of femininity and the implications for higher education access and choice are explored. Importantly, the chapter identifies that maintaining and shaping women's femininity and decision making about higher education are shared processes – and how the two intertwine. The shared social process of higher-education decision-making defies notions of autonomous rational choice for young people who are considering higher education access and choice (Thomas, 2021): 'decision-making [about higher education] is not an unfettered process – an exercise in free will and agency – but, rather, it is embedded within pre-existing societal structures underpinned by fundamental inequalities' (Brooks & Waters, 2021, p. 16). Family members are heavily involved in higher education access and choice across country contexts, but Haryana emerges as a particularly clear example of family – particularly parental – involvement. In our study, the role of others also emerged as strongly relevant as the young people and their

58 Honour and marriage

family members were advised by and consulted others about the mysterious process of accessing higher education. Higher education decision-making involves multiple stages, including deciding whether or not to attend higher education, choice of institution and selection of course/subject. There is the potential for codes of femininity to play out in each of these stages, as we go on to show in the sections of this chapter.

The chapter moves through two major sections, based on key aspects of femininity and how they relate to higher education access and choice. First, the notion of honour is explored, and the attached concepts of risk and safety are then applied to higher education access and choice. Second, the chapter addresses the practice of marriage, and how higher education interacts with this practice in different ways, including higher education being perceived as detrimental or advantageous for young women's marriage prospects. The chapter shows the ways in which resistance and transgression emerged in our study with regards to young women's higher education access and choice.

4.2 Honour and safety – higher education as risk for young women

4.2.1 Honour, safety and risk

The association of women with honour – and the risk of an unmarried woman's honour being 'spoilt' – is common across many country contexts. Women in India and in particular Haryana do not just bear their own honour (*'izzat'*), but they also contain the family's – and even the community's – honour within their bodies (Chowdhry, 1993, 2004a). Honour in this case refers to chastity and purity. To spell out chastity and purity, the expectation upon a woman is virginity, not only in the sense of not having penetrative sex before marriage but also in the sense of not even being tainted with traces of romance or desire (Chowdhry, 2004b). Family reputation is closely linked with honour, and where a young woman is reputed to be associating with men in a social way or having romantic liaisons, there is a risk of rumours spreading and the reputation being considered at risk or even already damaged. In Haryana, the honour narrative is strongly present and indeed comes to govern much of young women's lives, as explored in this chapter. A widespread fear is that a young woman associating with young men increases the chances of her eloping with a groom of her choice. The consequences for family honour, particularly one where the marriage is between two social groups which are not supposed to intermarry, are perceived as devastating (Chowdhry, 2007).

A hugely limiting factor on young women's lives is that honour and reputation can be damaged without any action on the part of the young woman. Sexual harassment in the form of 'eve teasing' (i.e. making lewd comments in the street), unwanted physical touching and sexual assault including rape are very common in Haryana (Preeti & Rajeshwari, 2018). When women are subjected to sexual harassment, they somehow pick up a share of the blame, and their honour is to a greater or lesser extent compromised. As we found in discussions with participants in our study, the media play a significant role in promoting panic about elopement and rape and the damage these cause to family reputation. Where reputation is considered to be damaged, this has repercussions for the family due to the compromised marriage prospects of younger siblings. Moreover, there can be other repercussions pertaining to the social status of the family and their positioning in society.

These issues translate into a very strong narrative relating to the maintenance of honour in the context of our study. The narrative is particularly visible in the limiting of young women's spatial mobility. The strategy that most families take for the protection of women's honour is a *prevention strategy*, in which responsibility falls on the young woman herself and her other family members, often brothers and cousin-brothers (Panchal et al., 2020), to prevent her honour from being spoilt and even to prevent rumours spreading about her, as in this account:

> We have a girl in our class who comes to tuition with me, and she tells us not to laugh a lot, as if by chance her brother observes it, he will scold her for it later.
>
> (Manisha)

The prevention strategy is commonly referred to in terms of *safety concerns* and keeping young women *safe*. Due to the preoccupation with safety, women's spatial mobility is constructed as *risky* and in need of risk management (Phadke, 2007), such as being accompanied, particularly by men from the family or, if necessary, by other women. It may prevent women's ability to go out at certain times, to certain places or indeed to go out at all (Chowdhry, 1999). It requires women to dress conservatively in 'suit-salwar of that type' (meaning traditional, modest dress) and to wear no make-up or 'clothes like jeans and tops' (i.e. Western clothes) (Kusum and Manisha). Not only are young men seen as threats, neighbourhood observers also constitute threats because they are capable of creating and spreading rumours about young women:

Interviewer: So, what the neighbours think makes a huge difference?
Babli: Yes ma'am.
Kusum, Ritu: It does not matter to *us*.
Kusum: It matters to parents.
Manisha: We just ignore it.
Kavita: It's just that, even if the parents don't think like that, if the neighbours come and tell [these things], and then they [parents] change their mind.

Depending on the reputed trustworthiness of the neighbour, interventions on the basis of rumour can be just as damaging as a real romantic liaison.

Young women in our study and other phases of our project (see Appendix A) discussed the importance of obtaining their parents' trust in order to access greater spatial mobility. This trust, which included relying on parents disregarding neighbourhood gossip, was built through demonstrating a flawless, serious attitude, which nevertheless could be threatened at any time:

> I have seen this about a girl [student], they [people in the neighbourhood] were saying that, 'I saw her going somewhere with somebody' and they were talking negatively about it, and they said that she should be married off.
>
> (Seema)

Participants sought out more positive media portrayals of successful women as a guide to their own pursuit of success. These included the film *Dangal* (a Bollywood film about a man with daughters who are sportswomen in North India, Tiwari, 2016); famous women such as Tina Dabi, who achieved first place for the Indian Administrative Service entrance examination (the famously competitive Indian civil service test) and Mary Kom, the Indian boxing star. Degrees of freedom were accordingly reflected in participants' responses. Rajvi noted that her parents allowed her to engage in many activities with NCC (National Cadet Corps) and to travel alone to college. Neetu stated that she had many boy/friends (in the friendship sense) and that her mother joked about it but did not find it problematic. Degrees of freedom can exist, as discussed by Oza (2019) in an article about women wrestlers in Haryana, who are accorded spatial freedom akin to that afforded to young men. Importantly, the price of this freedom, as discussed by Oza, is enhanced public suspicion and the requirement to maintain a flawless reputation along the way (see also Hussain, 2021, in relation to Assam).

How, then, does all this relate to higher education access and choice? Attending higher education is a spatial decision as well as a decision taken across many different axes of social life. For young women, higher education requires two significant steps which challenge the codes of safety and risk. First, attending higher education involves young women *going out*. The journey to college itself – which is, as we know, a daily occurrence for these students who are living at home while studying – is fraught with risk. Second, attending higher education also involves *inhabiting an unfamiliar space*. Going out for several hours to an educational establishment, where different social groups and different genders are mixing (in co-educational colleges) at an age when any suggestion of desire is seen as a heightened risk, presents a major source of fear for families, particularly if there is no direct experience of higher education in the family. This section of the chapter addresses the relationship between codes of femininity and specific issues of higher education access and choice, first in relation to the journey to college and second in relation to campus safety.

4.2.2 Commuting to and studying at college as risky endeavours

Here, we explore the perceptions of risk that are attached to travelling to and studying at college and consider how these risks intersect with higher education access and choice. A first important issue to explain is that, for some families, the idea of sending their daughters out to higher education was unthinkable. This was because colleges were located outside of the acceptable geographical horizon for young women (see also Narwana, 2019). Participants in our study referred to the fact that some parents are reluctant for their offspring to access higher education due to colleges being 'outside'. 'Outside' (*bahar* in Hindi) is a subjective marker; for some families, 'outside' refers to anywhere outside the direct place of residence (even within a zone of just a few streets beyond the household, where the family is known), and for others 'outside' refers to a college that necessitates taking accommodation elsewhere. Thus, for some families, the government colleges sampled in our study were themselves 'outside' (and thus inaccessible), and for others these colleges were *not* considered 'outside' or were deemed to be *less* 'outside' than others (so were preferable). The thinking behind this excerpt is explained by the SDC College Representative:

> Girls cannot be sent too far. This is a factor . . . this is a social thinking. They [families] think it is not right that girls go far from home. It is this; [they think] that, 'As they are close to us, they will remain in our control'. The times are such that they think this way, and [they think], 'Our social reputation should not be spoilt'.

A survey respondent similarly noted that young women do not access higher education 'because their parents do not agree, because there is nobody accompanying them and they do not want to send the girl outside' (SIDC, ID:7059). Another respondent stated:

> Some students did not get enrolled as they are from the village, and the thinking of people in villages is old-fashioned and they don't let their daughters go outside, and often get them married very fast. They think it's wrong to send girls outside. My female friends were very interested [in higher education], but due to family pressure they do not go to college.
> (SDC, ID:9103)

As discussed in Chapter 3, geographical horizons for young women were tighter than for young men. Young women in the massification generation were pushing at the limits of perceived acceptable spatial mobility for young women (Panchal et al., 2020), and still many women of this generation were leaving formal education during or after schooling. They were described by several participants as 'sitting at home' waiting for marriage.

While for some families accessing a college exceeded acceptable geographical horizons in terms of posing a risk to a young woman's honour, other families were prepared to send their daughters to the nearest college (which was for them not seen as 'outside'). This was not necessarily the college that their daughters would have chosen, and here the familial scope of the decision-making process becomes salient:

> Since there were never any educated girls [before], they [the family] did not want to send [me] *outside*. My maternal grandmother remarked that, 'She is a girl, and what special study will she do *outside*?' and that, 'If she wants [to study], she can study *here* [at MDC]'.
>
> (Reena, emphasis added)

> We had thought that we will get good knowledge if we go *outside*, so if we went *outside* we will learn something and become something ... So this has been the difference now that we are *not in the college of our liking*.
>
> (Reena, emphasis added)

Indeed, we saw that, in all three of the sampled colleges, the women students had gained a higher mean score between 4% and 8%, depending on the college, in their high school (Class 12) examinations than men students. This may indicate that young men with higher marks from these families and communities may have accessed more selective institutions, with young women accessing institutions closer to home, given we know this to be the case in other studies in other locations such as Delhi (Borker, 2021; Gautam, 2015). This argument is corroborated by a comment from one of the study participants, who noted that 'boys get it [permission to study outside] easily; we [girls] have to put a little pressure on parents' (Ritu).

In some instances, older members of the massification generation were already contributing to opening up the notion of 'outside' for younger sisters. For example Seema's older sister was studying for an MA at the nearby women's college; before she had accessed higher education, young women were not sent beyond the village for education. According to this participant, the older sister had changed the mindset of the village, meaning that the association of wider spatial mobility with inappropriate femininity had been altered.

Once permission has been granted to attend higher education, the daily commute to college represents a range of risks. The risk of bus travel for young women was recognised as a deterrent to families sending their daughters to higher education due to the prevalence of sexual harassment in buses which took the form of comments and touching in the always-crowded vehicles. Travel by *scooty* (i.e. moped/scooter) seemed to be a compromise that more financially comfortable families were trying out. Scooters, a relatively inexpensive form of personalised transport, allowed young women to travel to college without the risk of harassment in the buses. Neetu lived in the same town as the college. She either travelled to college on foot for ten minutes or by scooter for five minutes; it is interesting to learn that she used a scooter even for such a short distance, within a small urban area, showing the preference for staying off the street as much as possible, given the risks of eve teasing and being followed or jostled when on foot (Devi & Rajeshwari, 2018). However, problems still occurred using scooters: Poonam also noted that, when young women use the scooter to go to college, boys 'come behind you and make fun and bump . . . it is not very safe'. As such, the scooter does not provide complete security to young women for their journey to college. Because of the risky nature of occupying public space for young women, there was no optimal mode of transport for the journey to college – instead, young women and their families focused on minimising risk.

Some participants in our study engaged in complex journeys to college which were portrayed as fraught with risk, understandably, given the common knowledge of incidents occurring on the way to school or college (Women against Sexual Violence and State Repression, 2014). For instance Rajvi lived in a village ten km from the college. She did not have a means of transport within the family. She noted that reaching college on time took substantial planning. Sometimes, she would take a jeep (a village-run shared transport service), or she would take the bus. She then had to walk two to three km alone from the bus stop to the college, a substantial distance for a woman to walk alone in this context. She said she knew her parents would step in if there were any issues on this stretch of the journey. Seema lived in a village 20 km from MDC. Her journey to college began with a three-kilometre walk at the start of the journey, followed by a bus journey. The walking part of the journey caused issues with neighbourhood gossip. Like Rajvi, Seema reported her mother saying that if something happens, then at that point she will do something. In both cases here, we can see that there is a plan of retrospective action – 'if something happens' – which alludes to retribution where prevention is impossible. Due to the high levels of neighbourhood scrutiny of appropriate femininity, and communal involvement in higher education decision making, these intrepid young women were being watched on all sides – for the upkeep of their own honour and their family's reputation and for the potential for younger women to follow in their footsteps, in terms of newly appropriate boundaries for feminine spatial mobility.

The journey to college was not the only concern for families considering sending their daughters 'outside' for college. Families were also worried about what happened *at college*. These fears were particularly acute where co-educational colleges were concerned. Our study focused on co-educational colleges in a context where families of the massification generation were tending to opt for government colleges that were the closest to home, meaning that sometimes a co-educational college was the only available option, even for more privileged families, that was within an acceptable commute or geographical area:

Interviewer:	So the [students] who come to this college are from government or private school?
Babli:	No, both.
Kavita:	They come from both because there is only this one college and *for those whose parents don't want to send them outside, this is the only option.*
(Participant unclear):	They say that, 'This is close [to home], and this is a college too [i.e. it must be equivalent to others]'.

(Emphasis added)

For some families, the fact that a co-educational college was the only option within reach meant that daughters were not permitted to access higher education. It is important to recall that many parents and senior family members of the massification generation have never set foot inside a higher education institution. Simultaneously, due to patterns of gender-segregated living in Haryana, the idea of a space which is designed for young women to mix with young men was unimaginable for many family members.

Attending college is perceived as risky in two ways. First, an incident may occur in the environs of the college which may start rumours or even involve rape or sexual contact; second, attending college may bring young women into contact with young men, leading to romantic liaisons with the risk of sexual contact and/or elopement. Participants referred to the phenomenon of 'loafing boys' (i.e. young men out of employment or not attending college) who hang around near colleges and cause issues for women (Women against Sexual Violence and State Repression, 2014). Satish noted: 'They [parents] sometimes refuse to allow girls to go to college as they are afraid that the girl will be trapped [in an affair] with a loafer'. A survey respondent wrote that families were afraid that their daughter's 'future will be ruined' (SDC, ID:7031). The concept of *mahaul*, which translates as 'environment', featured in relation to women's safety at college. Participants discussed that some colleges gained a reputation as having an unsafe *mahaul*, with heightened risk to a woman's honour. For instance a survey respondent noted 'There [at a college] boys and girls romance each other and study less' (SDC, ID:9018). *Mahaul* was a contributing factor for the choice of college for young women:

Kavita:	The environment there is also like that, because of which I did not enrol there.
Interviewer:	What do you mean by environment?
Kusum:	There are boys there, who taunt and tease.

Honour and marriage 65

In addition to a college gaining a reputation as having a risky *mahaul*, there were also discussions of specific parts of colleges bearing risk. At MDC, women students were in a minority, and it was unclear where it was safe for them to spend time between classes and during breaks. They discussed that they felt unable to occupy spaces within the college grounds (see Figure 4.1 for an example of college grounds):

> I had thought to start a new practice [of girls using the space of the campus to sit and hang out]. But then a lot of girls told me that the environment inside the campus is not nice.
>
> (Seema)

Environment in this sense was not mentioned for young men in relation to college choice or in relation to occupying space within a college. Not having access to *all parts* of a higher education institution is a feature of the way in which partial access to higher education is granted to those who are seen as 'outsiders' in higher education (Iverson, 2012). One consequence of this is that many women's colleges are being opened in Haryana as a means of allowing women to access higher education in a safe and protected environment, that is with reduced risk of young women's honour being damaged

Figure 4.1 The Grounds of a Government College in Haryana
Source: the research team

(Verma, 2014). A critique of this approach was aired by the SDC College Representative:

> [T]here are now so many girls' colleges being opened by the government, *which is wrong*. Then parents think that the girl will only go to the girls' college and boys to the boys' [i.e. the co-educational] college. Yes, girls can go to the boys' colleges, but they [parents] do not send them because there are boys there . . . According to our society, the girls should not be exposed to boys a lot as they could get spoilt. They [parents] are worried that she might bring dishonour to their name.
>
> (Emphasis added)

Concerns relating to honour, safety and risk are interwoven in complex ways in individuals' accounts of their higher education choices. From the interview accounts with women students, we can see how particular choices were made.

Rajvi took a gap year between Class 12 and enrolling in higher education and took a computing course during that year. She learned about the college from a friend who was already enrolled in the college and who spoke positively of her decision. Her parents supported her decision but did not advise on college choice. Her older sisters (who had not attended higher education) asked why she was studying so much and asked why she was not getting married. She chose her college because she did not want to attend a college that was far from her family – and for her, 'far' was the urban centre of the neighbouring district. She did not consider another nearby college due to its reputation for 'cheap types' and 'incidents', so SDC was in this sense the only option. She felt it was safer to be at SDC because her sister lived in the same town as the college, so if she had issues she could get assistance.

Neetu chose SDC because it was near to her house. She had been advised to go to a college with at least some status, and she had thought about applying to a relatively prestigious university elsewhere in the state. She had also considered another college, and her brother was encouraging her with this, but it would have necessitated staying in a student hostel and she did not want to stay outside of the home. Also, she had visited the hostel and felt the facilities were too basic. She did not want to be far from home because she was the youngest child and was used to lots of love and affection from her family. If travel had been easier to the other college, she could have commuted, but she was worried about issues and bad comments. In the end, she only filled in the admissions form for SDC. All of her siblings had attended SDC.

Seema chose MDC because this was the closest college to home. It was also a mixed-gender college, and she was a strong believer in co-educational higher education.

Rajni had achieved her JBT (Junior Basic Training – teaching qualification) after Class 12 from a college near the district urban centre and stated that she had chosen her own college. She had considered going to the women's college near MDC, but they did not offer the course she wanted to take, so MDC was the only option. She stated that she wanted to go to college from 'here' (i.e. staying at home).

From these accounts of higher education choice, and from the section at large, we can see glimpses of different lives unfolding, young people making decisions about their futures drawing on different sources of guidance and with different degrees of autonomy and agency. Despite all of the nuances, all of these women selected a college that was close to home. Whether this is expressed as preference or obligation, as only one option or as an option among many, there is a sense that, for these women, *accessing higher education was in some ways limited to selecting the nearest college*. Bound up in distance and proximity is the protection of young, unmarried women's honour; for most of these massification generation students, they were breaking existing, community-accepted spatial boundaries. As a result, they were testing boundaries of appropriate feminine behaviour. Families were then trying to make sense of all this change and unfamiliarity within limited financial means, meaning that only some of the perceived risks could be mitigated. Higher education access for these young women was indeed a leap of faith; as they travelled to and from college and studied within college grounds, they bore the burden of their own and their families' honour with them at every step.

4.3 Higher education and marriage

4.3.1 Marriage, family and investment

Familial expectations of (heterosexual) marriage as a future prospect feature in young people's imagined trajectories in Haryana, irrespective of gender. However, marriage has a different significance for young men and young women and, as such, feeds into norms of femininity and masculinity in different ways. Here, we focus on the significance of marriage for women, and how marriage intersects with higher education access and choice; we address masculinity and higher education in Chapter 5. As with the discussions of honour and femininity in the previous section, when setting out dominant social norms it is important to recall that these are *norms*, which by definition are not necessarily followed or followed in the same way. Norms surrounding marriage are interpreted differently in different families and communities in Haryana and across India. While many of the nuances of marriage in Haryana may not apply across country contexts, many of the wider norms and social meanings of marriage – and the ways in which they intersect with higher education access and choice – do apply more widely. Furthermore, simply recognising how young people's future plans about higher education tie into their future expectations about relationships and life prospects is a valuable – and often neglected – consideration for higher education research globally.

68 Honour and marriage

A perhaps rather obvious statement to make, given the context, is that there is an assumption that marriage will be part of a woman's life and indeed that it is a (if not *the*) major purpose of her life, along with having children (in particular *sons*). As such, ideals of marriageability are inextricably intertwined with femininity, and young women's lives before marriage are shaped by their responsibility to protect, if possible to enhance, and definitely not to deplete, their marriageability. Marriageability is predicated on a young woman and her family having a sound reputation; marriages of offspring contribute to maintaining or enhancing the family's standing in society. Spoilt honour leads to a tricky search for a groom, potentially a compromise in terms of the groom's family standing and a potential reduction in social standing of the family at large – with associated subsequent issues for the marriage of younger siblings.

An important consideration when discussing marriage in Haryana is that marriage is a family matter. Marriage unites two families via two individuals, and young people are brought up with a strong awareness of their families' expectations about their future match. There are clear codes in place relating to religion (marrying within the same faith) and caste. Spouses are generally sought and approved by families in forms of arranged marriages that incorporate more or less active engagement with the couple themselves. While love marriages are not unheard of, even the notion of a love marriage generally occurs within the appropriate caste-related practices. The caste rules are particularly intricate, where there is an expectation of marrying within the same caste group but simultaneously an expectation of exogamous marriage, that is not within the same familial line (marked by *gotra*) or village. A family's fears around marriage are activated by rumours of elopements between young men and women from different caste groups or from the same *gotra* (Chowdhry, 2004a, 2004b).

With the birth of a girl child, the family is immediately aware of the future financial *burden* of her wedding, as well as the *risk* attached to protecting her honour until marriage. Sunil explained the tradition of celebrating the birth of a girl and a boy differently. With a boy child, he stated that 'there are celebrations, [they] will call a DJ and hold a party in the village', while if a girl is born, they say that 'they have a stone with them', that is a burden. We saw in the previous section that women's spatial mobility was curbed by women's families and that practices of chaperoning were also common. These restrictions and practices of accompanying women to protect them feed into the collective protection of an unmarried woman's honour. Decision making about young women's actions – including higher education access and choice – was a collective process, given that there is the potential for rumour to spread in relation to any micro-level actions that young women are seen to be performing, including simply being seen walking somewhere.

In addition to a girl child representing a financial burden and a risk to the family's honour, there is further consideration around family investment in daughters. Because of the patrilocal tradition where daughters leave the family home when they are married – and the location of the family home due to exogamous practices – and join their in-laws in the *sasural* (marital home) (Mukhopadhyay & Seymour, 1994), there is a common consensus that daughters are with their birth families in a temporary, transient manner. When they marry, they become the responsibility of their in-laws and also will contribute their labour (paid and/or unpaid) to their marital family. This means that investment in daughters is geared towards the moment of marriage, rather than towards their long-term prospects (Chakrabarti, 2009).

These dominant norms around femininity in relation to marriage have a great deal of salience for higher education access and choice. Higher education poses risks to honour, as discussed in the previous section, and moreover attending higher education can introduce young women to young men who are perceived as a threat to her marriage prospects. Higher education also requires investment from the birth family in various ways, which feeds into the questions a family will be asking itself about returns on investment. In the next section, we unpack the various different intersections between marriage and higher education in relation to dominant codes of femininity.

4.3.2 Intersections between higher education and marriageability

The relationship between higher education access and choice and marriageability is complex and multifaceted. In this section, we set out various complexities relating to how higher education can be seen. The section reveals that marriageability is constructed in relation to higher education access and choice in ways that are layered with dominant norms of femininity.

Higher education as not enhancing or depleting marriageability

In Chapter 3, we saw that, in many families, the previous generation of women to the massification generation was often educated to a generation behind the education levels of men in the family. This meant that, for young women, attending higher education marked a huge generational leap, whereas for young men higher education often represented a logical next step for generational social mobility. Thus, in terms of logical expectations for young women of the massification generation, completing secondary school or high school marked a reasonable step up from previous generations. Members of previous generations felt that higher education represented *too much education* for young women:

Ritu: My paternal aunt had refused [that I go to college], saying that, 'You have completed Class 12 [end of high school] so stay at home'.
Kavita: My whole family is [talking] like this.

Progressing beyond schooling was seen as a wasted investment and potentially even a risk to marriageability if the young woman would be perceived as too educated by potential grooms' families (Bhog & Mullick, 2015). Seema stated that, in the social norms, the men are the principal breadwinners, and education is intertwined with employment prospects, meaning that investing time and money into a woman's education is wasted:

> They [family members] say that, 'What will she do after study: there is only one person who earns'. So they did not educate her because they did not want her to do a job later on . . . They never wanted her to do a job, so what will she do with education.
>
> In the village what happens is, when a girl starts going outside, they will say 'Look your daughter is going outside, how much will you educate her? After all, she only has to do housework'.

Investment in a daughter's education was also intertwined with the future wedding costs, as delaying marriage in order to complete higher education requires further financial investment in the young woman, in terms of direct costs and living expenses. If higher education is considered unnecessary or even too much for a woman, the returns on this investment are slim and require a different understanding of the value of the girl child in the family than has been the tradition. Wedding costs weighed heavily on students' families, whom, as we know, were not economically privileged. In the FGD with women students at MDC, one of the participants was married. In her family, there had been pressure for multiple siblings to marry at the same time to save on wedding costs (see also Panchal et al., 2020). Finally, as we have seen, accessing higher education and consequentially delaying marriage entailed risks of a young woman's honour being spoiled or of her eloping. Amit said that some families prefer to marry their daughters off after schooling due to safety issues and the risk of elopement.

Waiting for marriage – higher education as 'time pass'

Some families – generally those which were more financially comfortable – were less in a hurry to marry their daughters. There was, as a result, a period of time to fill in these young women's lives. This period of time was associated with risk due to the young woman being of a marriageable age but not meaningfully occupied. Families with daughters in this position were weighing up contradictory risks: to keep the daughter at home, where she would hopefully not come into contact with young men and would not push at acceptable boundaries of spatial mobility but could get into mischief anyway? Or, to send the daughter to college, where she would be at risk of her honour being spoilt on the commute and while at college, but she would at least be meaningfully engaged in further study, which would also potentially contribute to her marriageability? Kusum stated that young women in this position come to college 'to get out of the house, to free the mind, to sit and drink tea and water, and go home'. In this intertwining of higher education access and marriageability, higher education has a clear function of 'time pass', which represents a gamble on higher education being *less risky* than the alternative option.

Higher education as enhancing marriageability

In other cases, higher education was considered as straightforwardly enhancing marriageability or even as required to make a good match (see also Verma, 2014). Again, this was associated with families which were more financially comfortable and which were targeting grooms who were themselves educated to high levels. Rajvi noted that at least an undergraduate degree was needed – because young men are educated these days, women have to be too. This was discussed in the SDC women's FGD, where the participants noted that a woman with a degree was more valued than a woman with school completion. Manisha quipped, 'they don't educate their own daughter but they want an educated daughter in law'. Importantly, this function of higher education as providing a qualification for marriage means that the *meaning of higher education* for women is shaped accordingly; for families in this position, sending their daughters to college was a *necessary risk* in order for the daughters to be matched according to the family's expectations. Higher education choice for these young women was shaped by the idea that the education itself was not considered particularly important, as it was not seen as a training *towards* a future occupation (other than being a wife and mother). Seeing higher education in this way means that the choices of institution or course of study are relatively unimportant, so that daughters may as well attend the nearest college to home, irrespective of their high school marks and preferences, and may as well select a course that is perceived as acceptable and/or manageable for women.

Higher education as a strategy to delay marriage

The young women in our study did not particularly relish the idea of marrying. Some participants expressed overt suspicion of marriage as a practice that brings trouble. As such, many young women were engaging in an active strategy of resistance against their families. They were negotiating with their parents to delay their marriage so that they could attend higher education (see also Thomas, 2021). The women's FGD at SDC also discussed that women can become more educated, self-confident and self-dependent by attending higher education. The participants argued that, previously, women were dependent on men for certain tasks such as filling in forms for various matters: 'now we can do it on our own' (Kavita); 'now if a lady earns she has some control' (Kusum). These remarks were accompanied with sounds of acquiescence from all participants. It is a recognised phenomenon that women with higher levels of education, especially degree-level qualifications, have more decision-making power in households (Mishra & Tripathi, 2011).

Parents *could* be swayed away from maintaining conservative norms around early marriage. For example Rajvi's parents, who had arranged her sisters' marriages at the ages of 16–17, had started to arrange her own marriage when she had just started higher education. In this case, the college principal intervened, in part because this student was well known as an NCC (National Cadet Corps) leader, and convinced them to allow her to continue with her studies. This had worked to postpone marriage plans, but her parents continued to discuss her marriage, particularly as her mother was unwell and wanted to marry this last daughter during her lifetime. It is important to note that using higher education as a strategy to delay marriage was only necessary for daughters from families where higher education was seen as not enhancing or was even seen as depleting marriageability; as discussed earlier, for other families, higher education was a family's preference in terms of waiting for marriage or enhancing marriageability. For daughters who were bargaining with their families to allow them to study, their presence in higher education was fragile and vulnerable to changes in family priorities (Bhog & Mullick, 2015), especially given the economic pressure on these families regarding wedding costs. These issues of bargaining and borrowed time were discussed in the SDC women's FGD, where Ritu stated: 'the day she stops studying and sits at home, they will get her married'.

Young women were reliant on older members of the massification generation (e.g. relatives, others in the community) to push at and extend the levels of appropriate educational and the boundaries of acceptable spatial mobility – and, as a result, to also set expectations about delaying marriage:

> It seems like only boys become something in our family and there are no educated girls, because of which I feel that, if one or two girls also become something, then it will be [the case] that, in our family, there is a girl in our family who can do something. For equality and to study.
> (Women's FGD, MDC, participant unclear)

Older sisters and brothers too emerged here as being extremely influential. For Neetu, she had an older sister who had achieved a BEd degree from SDC and a double MA from a college in another district, and she was still studying. Her second older sister was also still studying – an MCom at SDC college. Her brother had finished an MCom at SDC and was teaching in another location in the district. Her third sister (also older) had completed a BEd and an MSc from the district urban centre and was also now teaching in another location in the district. This extraordinary array of qualifications – and prior experience of SDC – provided this participant with a wealth of information from within her generation to support her own journey towards accessing higher education. Seema had an older sister who was studying for an MA in the nearby women's college. According to the participant, her sister was not interested in teaching but was just continuing with studies to defer marriage. She referred to her sister as having set the trend for the village. Rajni was following a precedent set by her sister, to wait until after her Master's to marry – she intended to use this precedent as a bargaining tool. Reena described the influence of her elder sisters. She described that she came from a low-earning household, that that there were seven siblings and that her older sisters set the trend of working, with all of them having taken jobs as teachers. She noted that this had encouraged her to apply for higher education. From these examples, we can see the sheer determination of members of the massification generation to extend educational possibilities for themselves and for their younger siblings.

Barriers to higher education once married

It is often assumed that higher education as a life stage slots in between schooling and an adult married life. While this is the dominant norm for accessing higher education, it is not necessarily the case that if a young woman marries after completing schooling, she will not be able to attend higher education. Some of the participants in our study were married – as noted, one FGD participant was married, and then in our survey 11 respondents were married and four were engaged to be married; these respondents were spread across genders and caste groups. Many participants discussed that members of their peer group were already married. However, there are a number of concerns that enter into view when considering the possibility of post-marriage higher education access. Due to the gendered power structures that shape women's lives, young women in Haryana are reliant on the goodwill of their birth families and then their marital families for their quality of life. Once married, a daughter-in-law is expected to take up significant labour in the marital home and cannot necessarily lay claim to her in-laws' financial resources to support her ongoing development (Bhog & Mullick, 2015). Even if the marital family provides permission and resources for further study, this does not necessarily mean that the daughter-in-law will be given relief from household duties or expectations of childbearing. Neetu stated that she did not have to do the housework, as her sister-in-law did this work, leaving her free to study. Parvesh noted 'They [women] get married first, so they cannot do [higher education]. For one thing their attention gets diverted to work at home'. One participant told a poignant story about her mother's higher education after marriage:

> My mother had come [to the marital home] after completing a BA and had started doing an MA. Since she had the burden of a lot of work, she failed a lot of times. My maternal uncle [who was supporting her to study] also started getting angry that he will not get her [re-enrolment] form filled if she wanted to keep studying. Poor thing she did not get time.
>
> (Manisha)

It was clear from the study that young women who were engaging in the resistance strategy of persuading their birth family to allow them to study before marriage were betting on a greater chance of completing higher education study before marriage, given the barriers to higher education study for a young woman once married.

Disconnect between marriageability and graduate employment aspirations

A final nuance to the relationship between marriageability and higher education access and choice that emerged in our study was a disconnect between the aforementioned connections between marriageability and higher education and the employment aspirations that young women in our study discussed. As noted at the start of this section, it must be remembered that, by definition, norms are not necessarily followed by all families and are interpreted and enacted in different ways. This book has so far set out a clear norm that women in Haryana are not expected to have a career and, in general, are expected to work within the home, including in family farms and businesses and running the household (Himanshi & Rajeshwari, 2021). However, an interesting norm emerged in our study of women discussing their employment aspirations in parallel with the discourse of compulsory marriage.

It was unclear the extent to which women were planning to work for a couple of years before marriage, or after marriage but before having children, or if they intended to maintain a career alongside their duties as a spouse. It may be that our study was charting social change in the making, in aspiration and expectation even if not in reality. For instance Poonam stated 'I want to do BSc, MSc, MPhil, PhD and get a job'; Seema aimed to become a school teacher with the help of her MSc and PhD degrees. For Poonam, her paternal uncle's daughter was influential as she was a professor at one of the universities in Haryana. She said she would go to her house sometimes and would feel encouraged by her cousin's life and her evident satisfaction. The role of women family members who were working in setting these expectations came through in our study. For Manisha, her paternal aunt had been influential. She was a school teacher and had told Manisha she should go to college; not only this, she had also encouraged another participant (Poonam) in the same vein, and the aunt's son was also helping them.

Several participants aimed to work in banking after completing higher education. Neela stated that banking is 'a good job; as soon as the BSc is finished there will be a job in hand'. She also stated that 'banking is better for girls' but did not explain this statement. However, there is perhaps some clue in Kamna's account, where she said that her own aspiration had been to become a lecturer, but her family had said that to complete further studies 'will be a little long, because of which the family is saying to go into banking sector as it is shorter'. There is an implication here of spending a shorter time working before marriage, whereas potentially a further degree would delay marriage further. Another clue to this gendered preference for banking occurred in relation to Neha, who had aspired to be a fashion designer. However, her mother was urging her to go into banking, as becoming a fashion designer would necessitate 'going outside' (here meaning living away from home) due to the limited scope for this work near her house. The FGD participants explained that there would be family anxiety if they stayed away from home in a place with an unknown environment.

Rajvi, who was an NCC leader, wanted to work in the army or police, though she preferred the police as this would allow her to live near her parents. She had wanted to be in the police since being a small child. She was aiming to prepare for the police service entrance exam after completing her degree. She said that her parents were supportive as they had wanted this for a son, but they did not have a son. She aspired to become their son. Initially, her father had wanted her to complete a nursing course to become a nurse; he was influenced in this by her friend who was doing this training. He had felt that nursing was a good job option for women and was unsure about women being in the police. He thought that women should have jobs that start in the morning and end in the afternoon, but she countered this by saying that nurses also work shifts. There were other family suggestions such as banking and fashion design. For this participant, her position as an NCC leader was an important means of extending spatial boundaries. It was not only considered respectable but also led to her travelling to different districts in the state and engaging in activities at the battalion and other places beyond the college. This young woman was an interesting mixture of dominant norms of femininity and masculinity in that, alongside NCC and preparing to enter into the police force as her parents' only 'son', she also engaged in more feminine-associated competitive singing and dancing and earned some money from singing for occasions and from sewing work.

There are a number of explanations for this disconnect between norms surrounding expedited marriage for young women and their employment aspirations. One explanation is that young women were citing emergent discourses that represented their hopes but not their prospects. Another explanation is that the strong social inequalities even within a relatively homogenous subgroup of the massification generation mean that at least some employment in the future is a concrete possibility for some young women but remains out of the question for others (Himanshi & Rajeshwari, 2021). A third explanation is that our study was picking up on a new set of generational social change for young women, with the boundaries of marriage – or, after marriage, of childrearing – being actively pushed back by this generation. It may be a shift in the concept of appropriate femininity now to contain at least a brief spell of working in the formal sector or as teachers in government or private schools.

4.4 Conclusion

This chapter has charted how dominant norms of femininity interact with higher education access and choice to shape the lives of young women in the massification generation in Haryana, India. At the same time, many of the norms set out in this chapter have salience – at least to some extent – in other parts of India and indeed internationally.

This chapter revealed that an unmarried woman's honour is also her family's honour and that protecting her honour up to the point of marriage is both her personal responsibility and also a family project. This project translates into a strategy of risk prevention which may restrict access to any higher education or which feeds into the choice of higher education institution. Particularly sensitive areas of risk are the commute to college and time spent at the college. For some families, these risks are mitigated by opting out of higher education, choosing online courses or selecting women's colleges. For other families, this risk assessment translates into choosing the nearest college and/ or a college with a commute that is considered safe.

A second major dimension of femininity included the clear association of women with marriage and the priority for a woman's marriage to maintain and if possible to enhance the family's status. Again, marriage is a family project, which translates into a shared responsibility across family members to fund the wedding and to maintain and if possible enhance the young woman's marriageability. The fact that women in this patrilocal tradition leave their birth family and their family's location upon marriage means that women are constructed as temporary household members, and investment is therefore directed towards marriageability. This investment may or may not include funding higher education. Higher education access and choice were shown to interact with marriageability in different ways. For some families, particularly those which are less well off, higher education may be constructed as too much education, as wasted investment or even as leading to an undesirable (over-educated) bride. Higher education also delays marriage, and this delay poses extra financial costs and potentially extra risks of a woman's honour being damaged during higher education. For other families, those which are more financially comfortable, higher education is a relatively safe and even worthwhile means of 'time pass' before marriage. Alternatively, higher education is seen as beneficial or even essential due to grooms' families' expectations of an educated bride. The chapter showed that higher education can be used by young women as an active strategy to delay marriage. This is a fragile and risky balance, but the possibility is strengthened by the presence of senior members of the massification generation who have already pushed at the boundaries of acceptable feminine behaviour in terms of level of education and spatial mobility for education purposes. The chapter showed that higher education before marriage is easier to obtain than after marriage, with marriage constituting a barrier due to the expectations of household labour that are placed on daughters-in-law. Indeed for some daughters, their higher education study time was possible due to their sisters-in-law doing the housework. Finally, there seemed to be a parallel discourse emerging about higher education as leading to employment for young women, and it is difficult to align this with the norms of women not participating in the formal workforce and of compulsory marriage. In our study, we seemed to be seeing some changes – at least at the level of aspiration – in the future prospects of young women of the massification generation.

Overall, this chapter argues that for young women from the massification generation, attending higher education represents a gender transgression in and of itself. Where femininity is bound up in honour and marriageability, higher education poses a whole new set of confusing risks and benefits for families in the massification generation. Attending higher education was a major generational leap in terms of women's educational attainment and spatial mobility. Arguably, this existential transgression left minimal space for further resistance and transgression. Women attending higher education had to compromise on multiple fronts, including a restricted choice of institution, irrespective of their academic potential or aspirations, and maintaining an impeccably studious reputation that inspired their parents' trust (see also Thomas, 2021). A major impression that emerges from this chapter is a sense of constraint, both within women's minds and bodies and externally imposed limitations. While many of the nuances of femininity and higher education access and choice presented in this chapter are specific to Haryana, and to the Indian context, notions of constraint and compromise are familiar as global traits of gender inequality. The next chapter goes on to explore how masculinity operates in relation to higher education access and choice, tracing through the norms that shape the lives and prospects of the future spouses of the women represented in this chapter.

References

Bhog, D., & Mullick, D. (2015). *Collectivizing girls for social change: Strategies from India*. American Jewish World Service's Early and Child Marriage Initiative. Retrieved June 30, 2023, from https://ajws.org/our-impact/measuring-success/research-early-child-marriage/collectivizing-girls-for-social-change

Borker, G. (2021). *Safety first: Perceived risk of street harassment and educational choices of women. Policy research working paper no. WPS9731*. World Bank. Retrieved June 26, 2023, from http://documents.worldbank.org/curated/en/723631626710146405/Safety-First-Perceived-Risk-of-Street-Harassment-and-Educational-Choices-of-Women

Brooks, R., & Waters, J. (2021). Decision-making: Spatio-temporal contexts of decision-making in education abroad. In A. C. Ogden, B. T. Streitwieser, & C. Van Mol (Eds.), *Education abroad: Bridging scholarship and practice* (pp. 15–27). Routledge.

Chakrabarti, A. (2009). Determinants of participation in higher education and choice of disciplines: Evidence from urban and rural Indian youth. *South Asia Economic Journal, 10*(2), 371–402.

Chowdhry, P. (1993). Persistence of a custom: Cultural centrality of Ghunghat. *Social Scientist*, *21*(9/11), 91–112. https://doi.org/10.2307/3520428

Chowdhry, P. (1999). Ideology, culture and hierarchy: Expenditure-consumption patterns in rural households. In K. Sangari & U. Chakravarti (Eds.), *From myths to markets: Essays on gender* (pp. 274–311). Manohar Publishers and Distributors.

Chowdhry, P. (2004a). Caste panchayats and the policing of marriage in Haryana: Enforcing kinship and territorial exogamy. *Contributions to Indian Sociology*, *38*(1–2), 1–42. https://doi.org/10.1177/006996670403800102

Chowdhry, P. (2004b). Private lives, state intervention: Cases of runaway marriage in rural North India. *Modern Asian Studies*, *38*(1), 55–84. https://doi.org/10.1017/S0026749X04001027

Chowdhry, P. (2007). Fluctuating fortunes of wives: Creeping rigidity in inter-caste marriages in the colonial period. *Indian Historical Review*, *34*(1), 210–243. https://doi.org/10.1177/037698360703400

Devi, P., & Rajeshwari. (2018). Violence against women in Haryana: Levels and correlates. *Punjab Geographer*, *14*, 52–64.

Gautam, M. (2015). Gender, subject choice and higher education in India: Exploring "choices" and "constraints" of women students. *Contemporary Education Dialogue*, *12*(1), 31–58. https://doi.org/10.1177/0973184914556865

Himanshi, Y., & Rajeshwari. (2021). Level of women work participation and its sociospatial dimensions in Haryana. *Demography India*, *50*(1), 139–151.

Hussain, S. (2021). Bhal Suwali, Bhal Ghor: Muslim families pursuing cultural authorization in contemporary Assam. *Gender and Education*, *33*(7), 830–846. https://doi.org/10.1080/09540253.2020.1773409

Iverson, S. V. (2012). Constructing outsiders: The discursive framing of access in university diversity policies. *The Review of Higher Education*, *35*(2), 149–177. https://doi.org/10.1353/rhe.2012.0013

Mishra, N. K., & Tripathi, T. (2011). Conceptualising women's agency, autonomy and empowerment. *Economic and Political Weekly*, *46*(11), 58–65.

Mukhopadhyay, C., & Seymour, S. (1994). Introduction and theoretical overview. In C. Mukhopadhyay (Ed.), *Women, education and family structure in India* (pp. 1–35). Westview Press.

Narwana, K. (2019). Hierarchies of access in schooling: An exploration of parental school choice in Haryana. *Millennial Asia*, *10*(2), 183–203. https://doi.org/10.1177/0976399619853720

Oza, R. (2019). Wrestling women: Caste and neoliberalism in rural Haryana. *Gender, Place & Culture*, *26*(4), 468–488. https://doi.org/10.1080/0966369X.2018.1502162

Panchal, T. J., Thusoo, S., & Ajgaonkar, V. (2020). Child marriages in Haryana: Challenges in implementing PCMA, 2006. *Economic and Political Weekly*, *55*(19), 58–64.

Phadke, S. (2007). Dangerous liaisons: Women and men: Risk and reputation in Mumbai. *Economic and Political Weekly*, *42*(17), 1510–1518.

Thomas, A. (2021). *The role of families in the gendered educational trajectories of undergraduate students in Haryana, India* [Unpublished PhD dissertation]. University of Warwick.

Tiwari, N. (Director). (2016). *Dangal* [Film]. Aamir Khan Productions and Walt Disney Pictures India.

Verma, S. (2014). Women in higher education in globalised India: The travails of inclusiveness and social equality. *Social Change, 44*(3), 371–400. https://doi.org/10.1177/0049085714536810

Women Against Sexual Violence and State Repression. (2014). *Speak! The truth is still alive: Land, caste and sexual violence against Dalit girls and women in Haryana*. Women Against Sexual Violence and State Repression.

5 Family responsibility
Masculinity and higher education access

5.1 Introduction

The previous chapter explored how dominant norms of femininity shape young women's higher education access and choice, ignoring the presence of young men. However, men remain *silent comparators*, where women are analysed as doing *more* or *less*, or being *more* or *less* – than what? By exploring women only, it is impossible to know to what extent men and other genders may share similar experiences. This chapter brings masculinity and young men's experiences to the fore, in order to give a comprehensive picture of how gender norms operate in relation to higher education access and choice, in Haryana, India and beyond. Importantly, as discussed in the previous chapter, masculinity is primarily attached to men and men's bodies, but its associations are also detached from bodies and affixed onto particular clothes, behaviours, even educational courses – and other gendered bodies. An important argument in this chapter is that attending higher education, including the associated spatial mobility, is in and of itself a masculine tradition with masculine associations.

In Chapter 4, we demonstrated that decision making around higher education is a shared social process within the family and maintained codes of femininity. Here, we show that families have a strong stake in what sons do and how their masculine social role is formed and enacted. It could be assumed from the previous chapter that men in Haryana enjoy a significant degree of freedom. There are certainly enhanced freedoms for young men in Haryana, which are explored in this chapter, but there are other constraints too, which are important to recognise, for their impact not only on young men's lives but also on women's lives, given the relationality discussed earlier. In this chapter, we see how young men's higher education access and choice are shaped by family pressures and by gendered roles within families, as well as how this positioning of young men impacts upon young women's higher education access and choice.

This chapter contains one major central section, which covers dominant masculinity norms and how they relate to higher education access and choice. In the first part of the section, the nuances of masculinity are explored, with

DOI: 10.4324/9781003331216-5

Family responsibility 81

specific reference to notions of family responsibility, employability and marriageability. In the second part, these notions are discussed in relation to higher education access and choice, particularly highlighting the impact that family responsibility may have on both. The section overall highlights that, for the massification generation in particular, higher education is perceived as risky for young men as well as for young women. As with the previous chapter, this chapter recognises that norms are norms, not universal descriptors of behaviour. Nuances and transgressions that push at the norms are threaded through this chapter. The chapter also weaves the norms of femininity discussed in the previous chapter together with these norms of masculinity.

5.2 Family responsibility – higher education as risk for young men

5.2.1 Family responsibility, employability and marriageability

In Haryana, as well as arguably in India more widely and indeed other country contexts, masculinity is constructed around the expectations of material provision. In particular, sons are required to support their parents and their siblings financially throughout their lives. In many families, especially in a context of economic deprivation, an expectation is placed on sons to help to fund their siblings' education, living costs and their sisters' wedding costs, which can be enormous due to the linking of wedding celebration displays with social status (Chowdhry, 1999). In Chapter 4, we highlighted that parents are known to celebrate the birth of a son and mourn that of a daughter, and Chapter 3 discussed dominant norms and practices of son preference. It is important to note that these practices do not rest on the intrinsic worth of a boy child, though this may appear to be the case. There is a strong instrumental rationale to son preference, which becomes intertwined with an appearance of intrinsic worth (Husain & Sarkar, 2011). Having a son is instrumentally beneficial because it assures the family line and family property in a system which is still heavily geared towards patrilineal inheritance and governed by the notion that sons will be financial providers for their families in the long term (Chowdhry, 1995). Therefore, for young men, investment in their education constitutes a long-term investment, accompanied by expected returns on the investment.

Unlike daughters, who are supposed to marry into a family which is located outside of her place of residence, outside of her village, and move away to join the marital family (Agarwal, 1994), sons are expected to stay close to (if not within) the family home and to take care of their birth families in financial terms. Young men are expected to prepare to support the family financially through their employment and to maintain their physical presence to oversee the family affairs (Narwana & Gill, 2020). These two dimensions of family responsibility sometimes collide in that there may be an opportunity to increase the earning potential by studying or working elsewhere. In such cases, where there is more than one brother in a family, one brother may choose to remain physically present and potentially forego a greater financial contribution.

In Chapter 4, we discussed that (heterosexual) marriage was understood as being *a* if not *the* major part of a woman's life. For men, this is also the case in terms of being *a* major part of life, but not *the* major part. A man's priorities is split between and enmeshed in wider family responsibility and employment. There is a clear assumption that marriage and having children – in particular a son and heir – are on the cards for young men as future prospects. Like women, men are also expected to maintain, enhance and not deplete their marriageability, but their marriageability does not take the same form as for women. For men, marriageability ties in with their employment prospects, and to a degree their educational achievements. There is an expectation placed on sons that they will become financially stable at the appropriate time in order to prepare for marriage. At that time, which again may vary across different social groups, they are expected to marry and bring a bride to the family home, who will then take care of the home and attend to the physical needs of the parents as they age. This is an important contribution and brings a source of labour to the home. As with women, love matches are not particularly welcome for men due to the importance of the family uniting with another appropriate family (Chowdhry, 2007). As noted in Chapter 4, an already-educated bride is preferred, and grooms' families carefully screen potential brides for the appropriate education level. A bride moving to the *sasural* then becomes the 'property' of the groom's family, not specifically the groom. Therefore, the choice of bride is not just an individual choice for the groom due to the wider ramifications of this choice for the family.

In Chapter 4, we discussed the heightened sense of risk that is associated with protecting young women's honour before marriage, and the notion that women must be kept 'safe' in order to protect from risks to their honour, including by restricting their spatial mobility. However, it is important to note that both honour and risk also govern men's lives, but the concepts have different meanings. Honour for young men is associated with maintaining and enhancing the family's social status and financial position and, as such, is not located within the body in the same way as women's honour. Honour for young men is not associated with chastity or sexual reputation; romance does not have a tainting effect to the same extent and may even be expected and imbued with masculine prowess. As noted by Chowdhry (2004b, p. 67), 'sex for an unmarried woman is severely condemned but for an unmarried man, it is not a matter to comment on'. For young men, since their honour is not contained within the body, then risk too is not located within their bodies. In terms of physical risk, men's bodies are not portrayed in the literature or in local parlance as being at risk from sexual harassment or violence. Men are always portrayed as the perpetrators of touching, groping and eve teasing, often as an implicit source of danger for women. Men do of course experience violence, but the physical risk to men's bodies is mainly associated with masculine violence between men. This can include gendered violence, where revenge is taken out upon the men of a family as a retaliation for an honour issue relating to a woman, or where men are trying to defend women and are attacked (Adur & Jha, 2018). This takes us back to the discussion of women's journeys to college in Chapter 4, where two participants referred to the fact that their families would act *if something happened*, implying the potential for revenge of some kind. In general, men's bodies are less protected than women's, with men being placed in more physically risky situations than women. Men are also expected to perform masculine roles of provider and protector which can involve a different kind of physical labour, placing them both as the source and target of violence.

For young men, then, risk to honour is not placed in the body but, rather, is located in the future. This means that the journey through young adulthood towards marriage is less fraught with honour-related risk for young men, as long as they make the right choices that will lead to supporting the family financially at the appropriate time. The appropriate time differs according to socio-economic status, being sooner for poorer families, and later, but with higher financial expectations, for richer families. We discussed the notion of parental trust in Chapter 4. For young women, trust meant maintaining a studious and impeccable reputation in order to permit the stretching of habitual spatial mobility and educational limits and the delaying of marriage. For young men, family trust was also a strong concern. Young men were more easily trusted, as trust, like honour, was not located in the body but rather in future financial provision. In our study, young men discussed relationships of mutual trust with their parents, alluding to open discussions with their parents and other family members about their future choices.

The location of honour, risk and trust outside of the body meant that young men were allowed relative freedom in terms of spatial mobility and educational access, as long as they were preparing in an appropriate way to support the family, or even already supporting it. It is important that we do not draw up a dichotomous distinction between young women's and young men's spatial freedom. It was not the case that no women were granted permission to go out of the house; women students in our study did discuss having fun outside, such as Neetu, who often went out to play cricket and marbles with her friends. It was, however, clear that young men were granted much greater spatial freedom than women in terms of place and time of day. Babli stated that young men 'can roam around until 8 or 9 pm; we [young women] cannot go anywhere', due to the suspicions that arise if young women go out in the evening. Parvesh reinforced this point, indicating that young men 'are given complete freedom, like an untethered buffalo'. Fear of elopement and the accompanying restriction of spatial mobility are associated more with women than men, even though in each (heterosexual) elopement, there is of course a man who has taken that path.

Due to the son preference practice of 'trying for a son', young men are more likely to occur later in the sibling birth order (see Section 3.3). However, brothers of any age are given substantial decision-making power within the family (Bhog & Mullick, 2015) and are held responsible to some degree for the protection of their sisters' honour and marriageability (Chowdhry, 2004a). They are expected to prevent their sisters from being harassed, from rumours spreading about them, from entering into romantic relationships and ultimately from their honour being spoiled (Chanana, 2001). Any of these occurrences may have serious implications for a brother's own marriage prospects and for the prospects of other siblings' marriages. Indeed, there are financial costs associated with a woman's so-called spoiled honour which may fall directly upon her brother/s; the marriage of a sister reputed to have spoiled honour may be more costly in terms of higher dowry payment or on expenditure related to lavish marriage arrangements. The masculine role of 'protecting' sisters leads to a situation where young men are often surveilling their sisters tightly and are also frequently engaged in chaperoning. In Chapter 4, we saw an instance where a brother would scold his sister if he saw her laughing and having fun outside of the home. If women are constrained within a discourse of keeping them *safe*, women's brothers are the agents deployed to keep them safe (Panchal et al., 2020). Moreover, this responsibility does not necessarily end with a sister's marriage – to some extent, brothers retain responsibility for their sisters after marriage, and the figure of the maternal uncle (the wife's brother and uncle to her children) is an important figure in married women's lives, including supporting and funding post-marriage higher education (Thomas, 2021; Chowdhry, 1997). Parvesh directly referred to the influence of his maternal uncle on his own higher education choices.

As discussed in the introduction to this chapter (see also Section 1.4), masculinity does not necessarily only attach to men's bodies. There was an important case in our study where Rajvi was taking on the role of son in her family (see also Section 4.3). She had three older sisters, with the eldest 15–20 years older than her; she was the child number seven in the birth order, as three other siblings had died at birth. With the eventual lack of sons in the family, she had become the son; as she stated, 'There are no brothers – I am the brother'. Rajvi had aspirations to join the police or military in order to support her family and also expressed expectations of maintaining physical presence close to her parents, to the extent that she preferred the police as this would involve more options to remain situated in one place (as opposed to the army, which imposes a more itinerant existence). Here, we see a woman placed in the role of son and expressing the dominant norms of the masculine social role (see also Oza, 2019). Unlike sons, daughters are in a sense dispensable due to their temporary existence within the birth family; we did not see any examples of sons taking on feminine social roles due to a lack of daughters.

Masculine gender norms around family responsibility mean that, for men, educational decisions are located in long-term future planning relating to their role as provider for the family. In the next section, we explore in more detail how these norms intersect with higher education access and choice.

5.2.2 Intersections between higher education and masculine family responsibility

In this section, we begin with the spatial dimensions of young men's higher education access and choice and then move on to consider different ways in which higher education decision making intersects with family responsibility priorities.

Spatial mobility and masculinity in higher education access and choice

Restrictions on spatial mobility with risk to honour did not apply to young men. This also meant that fears about the journey to college were less fraught, although young men were placed at physical risk by being obliged to sit on the roof of over-crowded bus services:

> There are a lot of problems in public transport: [buses] are always running full, there is a lot of crowd in the buses, boys even go on the roof of the buses; this is a very pitiable thing in today's time.
>
> (College Representative, SDC)

Men appeared in accounts of the journey to college as perpetrators of harassment – eve teasing, touching and groping in buses, bumping scooters. However, this does not mean that men were exempted from gendered spatial mobility concerns. There were three ways in which dominant norms of masculinity translated into spatial aspects of higher education decision-making: (i) the obligation of maintaining physical presence within the family home, (ii) awareness of and imbrication in the household finances and (iii) the requirement to maximise earning potential. These three concerns were not always aligned.

In our study, given our focus on government colleges in small urban centres, the young men had, in a similar way to young women, for the most part chosen the closest college to home. But this choice was made to prioritise the physical presence of sons within the household, with young men maintaining their presence in the home, including participation in decision-making processes and surveillance of sisters.

Second, choosing the closest college to home was related to household finances in terms of avoiding substantial commuting costs and/or accommodation costs:

> Like this [if attending a college that is further away] the facilities [at the college] and transport facilities will be wasted if we go far: time, money and your creativity [will be wasted].
>
> (Rahul)

86 Family responsibility

Young people who enrol in government colleges do not tend to originate from economically privileged backgrounds. From a young age, sons are prepared for their future role as financial providers by being included in discussions about the financial status of the family. While affordability and financial constraints appeared in most if not all of the young people's accounts of higher education choice, in young men's accounts, there was a particular sense of collective involvement in the family finances. For young women, it seemed to be a case of asking parents and being turned down; for young men, there was an implication that the young men had made the assessment by themselves (to an extent) in view of their understanding of the family's economic situation.

Third, young men from different social groups faced different concerns in relation to college choice (discussed further in the following sections). In spatial terms, there was at times a conflict between the responsibilities to maintain physical presence and not to drain family finances and the responsibility to maximise future earning potential. Choosing a college that was further away would potentially negate the first two responsibilities but could potentially enhance the third. Here, then, contradictory priorities arose in young men's higher education choices. Moreover, different and sometimes contradictory sources of advice appear in the young men's accounts. The young men seemed to be very aware that 'high quality' higher education could only be obtained by accessing colleges that were further from home, but at the same time Kaushal had been advised by a teacher that 'graduation [undergraduate degree] can be done from anywhere, while post-graduation [Master's level study] requires more attention [to the institution]'. In our study, young men were more likely than young women to have chosen their college based on some aspect of academic reputation, with men more engaged in discussing the quality of the education than young women. This may be attributed to the fact that the purpose of higher education was different, as discussed in Chapter 4; for young men, higher education was expected to lead to employment and to deliver financial returns on the investment of time and money, perhaps leading to a different assessment of higher education options.

The college choice narratives of the interview participants in our study revealed the interweaving of these three aspects of the spatial dimensions of higher education choice for young men.

Ravinder selected SDC because his older brother's friends were studying there and gave a positive review of the college. His older brother lived in Delhi, so he felt he should stay at home for his higher education. He had applied to SDC and another college in the district centre of another district and gained admission in both. He had attended a selective residential state secondary school, so had already experienced staying outside for education. However, he ultimately chose to attend SDC so he could stay at home and commute, stating that the college had low fees and a good level of education.

Sachin selected SDC because of his strong interest in NCC and because science was offered. Since NCC was a major factor in his college choice, he only had two options – SDC and the college in the district urban centre, which were both government colleges whose lower fees appealed to him, considering his family income. By travelling to the other college to see if his name was on the acceptance list, he also realised how challenging the commute would be. He discovered that, given the commute, he would have to consider a hostel, and he reasoned that this would involve even more costs, such as buying food rather than eating at home. This would have reduced the funds for his boxing practice, and he was planning to try to become a professional boxer. Finally, he had learned that the science education was of good quality at SDC.

Vikas' only option was MDC, based on family financial resources. He was content with this choice because it was close to home, and there was a half-hourly bus service that he could use to reach the college. He considered another college, but the public transport links were not efficient. His cousin had attended MDC and had given a positive review of the college and the commute, and his parents encouraged him to trust in his own instinct about this decision.

Amit had chosen MDC because, despite their wishes to send him to a 'good' college, his parents could not afford a private college. Moreover, attending another college would have necessitated staying 'outside' – he chose MDC in order to remain at home. He felt it was his responsibility to see what was affordable within the family's means. He preferred to attend a government college, as it was known that some private colleges were providing fraudulent degrees. He referred to not having substantial knowledge about college choice but had known seniors who had attended MDC, so they had specific knowledge of the college. He had also lived in the town where MDC was located since his childhood, so the family felt they had some local knowledge of the institution.

From these four narratives, we can see the ways in which the three spatial dimensions of higher education choice play out in terms of masculine notions of family responsibility.

In the previous chapter, we discussed that *being at college* (in addition to the commute) was also considered a risk for young women. This was not a concern for young men. There was no trend to seek out single-sex institutions for young men, although, as we have seen, co-educational colleges were becoming men's colleges by default, with a small number of women who were targeting particular subjects (particularly sciences). There was no discourse present in our study of families worrying about which women their sons were mixing with, no 'loafers' who were women. In terms of the risks to young women on campus, we discussed the notion of *mahaul* or 'environment' in the previous chapter. As with the journey to college, there is a sense of a masculine threat in the notion of 'environment', caused by the presence of men. This fits in with the idea that higher education spaces are inherently masculine spaces, given they were designed by and for men, with women coming up against a collective and pervasive sense of masculinity. Thinking about the concept of *mahaul* through the lens of masculinity rather than femininity leads us to ask – whose

88 *Family responsibility*

sons are these? Who is creating a bad environment and how? There is somehow always a sense of 'someone else's son or brother' being the perpetrator.

Different intersections between higher education and masculine family responsibility

In Chapter 4, we looked at higher education through a prism of marriageability. In this chapter, we trace through equivalent concerns for young men for several of these constructions of higher education. What we did not see in our study was any account of young men facing barriers to higher education after marriage. It is possible that these barriers did exist in terms of expectations placed on young men to support the family after marriage, but they were not evident. We also did not see the same disconnect between aspirations and likely trajectories for graduate employment that young women revealed. A different disconnect emerged in young men's graduate education aspirations.

Higher education as not enhancing or depleting enactment of family responsibility

In Chapter 4, we saw that higher education is perceived by some as being too much education for women, as constituting a wasted investment, an unnecessary and risky delay to marriage and potentially a depletion of marriageability. There are equivalent concerns for young men's prospects in that if young men are not expected to engage in higher education, and women are expected to be less qualified than their husbands, then the fact of men not accessing higher education has a direct impact on women's expected educational attainment. In Haryana, masculinity as a cultural norm is embedded in agricultural, sports and military prowess rather than in academic achievement (Chowdhry, 1986). This can in part be attributed to the way in which colonisation occurred in Haryana, where the British rule maintained Haryana as an agricultural state (ibid.). In the massification generation, particularly in first-generation students' families, higher education can be seen as somewhat mysterious and possibly pointless and as imposing a delay in sons' financial contributions to the family economy. Sachin explained that people had the mentality that higher education may lead to unemployment, so the preference was that finishing Class 12 (high school) was sufficient. This attitude was illustrated by Parvesh:

> Parents think, '[Boys] have done Class 12, do some work and earn 8,000–10,000 [INR]' . . . Here there is no value to graduation [an undergraduate degree] . . . And they say that, 'You go for a government job'; after Class 12 they ask you to start coaching: 'Leave everything with study and do coaching for the government services. Get a government job, [then, just] sit and eat [i.e. have a comfortable life]'.

Sachin also explained that, in Haryana culture, dropping out of sports was sometimes considered more serious than dropping out of education.

Opposition to higher education was more common in more socio-economically disadvantaged families, where there was greater pressure for sons to earn to support the family; this was also found in a study of neighbouring Punjab (Narwana & Gill, 2020). Seema mentioned that sons may be obliged to seek employment after Class 12 to finance a sister's wedding; Kaushal referred to pressures on older siblings to fund younger siblings' education. Already, attending high school had pushed back the age of earning for these young men to a later stage than previous generations, so the pressure to earn coincided with the moment of attending higher education for them. Narratives of the collision between education and the pressure to earn featured in participants' stories of previous generations of their families. For instance Rajvi's father had studied until Class 8 (lower secondary school). He had been obliged to begin work at that point, as his own father had died and he had to pay off the family debts. Amit explained that he came from a family of tailors. His maternal grandfather was a tailor who could not afford to send Amit's mother, maternal uncle or maternal aunt to school; his paternal grandfather was also a tailor who could not afford to educate the six siblings. His father had had no choice but to go into the family business. Amit went on to explain that he was aware of several of his peers who had not accessed higher education. He said that one friend had entered the army; others were doing labouring jobs and harvest work. He attributed this to young people not having parents or having sick parents who were not able to work, so they had to work to support the family, or to parents telling their offspring to stop studying or to parents being too poor to pay for the college costs. He also noted that other families had farms or businesses that their children could enter into without going to college.

There were two alternatives to higher education. In some cases, young men were discouraged from pursuing higher education in favour of vocational courses, which were shorter and had clearer employability prospects than higher education degrees. Harish's family had asked him to take a vocational course after Class 12, as it would only take two years to complete. In other cases, young men were expected to seek a job directly from Class 12. These included government jobs in the civil service, police and military, as well as taking up positions of responsibility in family businesses. There was also evidence of attrition of young men from higher education courses. One participant in our study noted that of the seven of his peers who had enrolled in higher education, he was the only one left. The women students had not dropped out. In Chapter 4, we discussed that some young women are withdrawn from higher education to be married off when the balance between education and marriage tips towards marriage; here, we see that, for young men, the balance between education and family financial contribution can tip towards financial contribution and can also lead to attrition from higher education.

Higher education as a parallel activity, akin to 'time pass'

In Chapter 4, we discussed that some young women were enrolling in higher education as a 'time pass' activity while waiting to reach an appropriate age of marriage. For young men, there was not the same sense of 'time pass' or waiting for marriage. However, there are some similarities: for young women, higher education was a parallel activity to waiting, and for young men, higher education was matched with engagement in other activities alongside higher education which included working or studying for entrance examinations for the civil service, military or police. In both cases, higher education was not considered the most important or the only thing that a young person of that age should be engaging in. For those who were working alongside studying, higher education accompanied the period where they were also moving into a position of responsibility within the family. Higher education seemed to represent a useful back-up plan or a signal of educational attainment to a potential bride's family (Thomas, 2021). There were discussions among participants in our study about students who were significantly engaged with their family businesses during their higher education study, including young men who had enrolled in distance higher education to permit them to spend more time working. A common phenomenon was the parallel engagement in a higher education course and coaching classes for entrance examinations. For graduate-level posts, both the undergraduate degree and success in the entrance examination were necessary. This resulted in some students choosing reputedly easier courses in order to cope with these parallel demands. One survey respondent wrote, 'I chose this course because I have to do coaching for a graduate-level post' (MDC, ID: 8036). For several students in our study, coaching was the priority, and higher education was designed to provide the back-up option of, for instance, becoming a school teacher (this was considered a 'government job', i.e. providing a stable, comfortable life). As discussed earlier, Sachin was training to become a professional boxer, in keeping with the elite sports culture in Haryana, and for him higher education was providing his back-up option of becoming a teacher. It is clear from across these accounts that young men are engaging in multiple activities to shore up their future (and in some cases current) role as providers within the family.

Higher education as enhancing the potential to enact family responsibility

In Chapter 4, we discussed the notion that higher education may enhance young women's marriageability or may even be a prerequisite within a social group to 'qualify' for a particular class of groom. With young men, likewise higher education may be seen as enhancing prospects in terms of family responsibility, especially as an employability enhancer (Gautam, 2015). This perception of higher education often accompanied a narrative of struggle in the parental generation. For instance Sachin recounted that his parents had told him about the poverty they had faced, and they were not encouraged or supported to study. He was therefore strongly encouraged to make the most of the opportunities, so that he would not struggle the way they had. From young men's narratives, the sense of family financial responsibility emerges strongly. Jatin stated that he wanted to complete higher education in order to 'support his parents in their old age'; Sunil stated 'in my family success has been a little low, when I achieve higher education through studying, I will uplift them in society'.

Just as a young woman's higher education choice was a shared family responsibility, there was a sense of young men's higher education choices also being taken in a collective decision-making process – and indeed sometimes of young men's own preferences not being considered. Rahul stated, 'my family wants me to study like this'. For Amit, both his mother and father encouraged him to study hard in order to prepare for the future. He was also encouraged by his maternal and paternal grandparents, his maternal aunt and his cousins. Family members said to him 'We could not study, but you should study'. Parvesh narrated a rather poignant tale, where his mother had obtained a BA and wanted to become an economics teacher. However, she had been 'quickly married and could not become one'. He noted that she had been 'a college topper' and still 'gets calls from the college'. Because she was unable to fulfil her ambition, she wanted her son to step into this opportunity and to excel as she had done. Fathers appeared in some of the qualitative data as being particularly involved in determining access to higher education of their progeny. Harish referred to his father's advice to him to enrol in MDC, which was based on the fact that he had himself attended the same college.

This sense of collective responsibility for a son's higher education choices played out in a lack of freedom to choose the course of study, which emerged in several accounts. Women's course choice was often limited by the expectations of studying whichever courses were available in the nearest college and the perception that the course was unimportant if the purpose of higher education was to prepare for marriage. For men, families were invested in their sons choosing a course with secure employment prospects. One survey respondent wrote, 'My father forced me to take admission in [this course]' (MDC, ID:8103). Different courses were positioned in a hierarchy: sciences at the top, followed by commerce, followed by arts; this was also found in a study of higher education subject choice of students enrolled in a university in Delhi (Gautam, 2015). This hierarchy was perpetuated in local discourse:

> [People say that] those who take science are good and those who take arts are good for nothing. And those who do not want to take arts, can take the middle ground of commerce.
>
> (Parvesh)

There was no interest [for me] in science and Maths. And the environment (*mahaul*) for arts is [not good] in our village. Arts is seen as useless; commerce is a bit ok.

(Naresh)

There was clearly more at stake in higher education choice for young men, in terms of the instrumental benefits of young men making the right choices to the family as a whole.

Higher education as a strategy to delay family responsibility

For young women, higher education was widely acknowledged as a strategy to delay marriage in families where the expected age of marriage conflicted with the age range covered by a conventional undergraduate degree. This discourse was almost absent for young men, in part because the urgency to marry was less intense at this age. However, there was one example of a young man, Ravinder, who referred to his family's urgency to arrange his marriage. They wanted him quickly to enter into a government job, and they would then arrange his marriage. He said he was trying to persuade his family to wait a few years more, in order to give him time to prepare for the many responsibilities that marriage brings. The pressure to assume family responsibilities and to finalise marriage plans did appear for young men in the study, but there was less evidence of higher education being used strategically to intervene in this pressure. Rather, men seemed to be busy establishing themselves as financial providers.

(Dis)connect between family responsibility and higher-education-related employment aspirations

In Chapter 4, we discussed a possible disconnect between young women's employment aspirations and the likely employment aspirations in a way that seemed to counter the expected trajectory of marriage and pregnancy immediately after graduating from college. We discussed different possible explanations for this: that their accounts represented hopes not real prospects; that employment was a prospect for more privileged students and that workforce participation (at least for a brief spell) was becoming a more common prospect for women in the massification generation. Young men were entering higher education with a much simpler relationship with future employment, in that employment was an obligation rather than a transgression. However, a different type of disconnect emerged in the young men's accounts; their narratives of their employment futures were often not straightforwardly connected with the higher education courses with which they were engaged. We have seen that young men were often studying at college as just one of their ongoing activities, as they moved into an adult role of masculine family responsibility.

For many, higher education did not feed directly into employability but rather represented an insurance option or a tick-box qualification. For example Sunil reported on the guidance he had received from his elder brother:

> He said that, 'Your qualifications begin with graduation, consider when forms [application forms for jobs] come out'. My aim is to be a police inspector [so he said], 'for that you need to be a graduate from any stream'.

There was a widespread recognition that attaining a higher education degree enabled 'forms to be filled', meaning an application to a graduate-level employment opportunity could be made, often regardless of the course or institution choice.

We have seen that for many young people in the massification generation, choices about higher education access and choice were based on hearsay and experiences of young people in the same generation, rather than direct experiences of higher education or graduate employment from previous generations, or reliable and accurate information on higher education options or career pathways. There was evidence of confusion among the young men in our study about how to ensure they were making the right choices to be able to support their families later on. Amit, who was also studying the BCom course, chose this course in order to become a Chartered Accountant via an MBA. After Class 10 (i.e. before high school), he had discussed with his parents which stream to take at high school (this has a strong bearing on options for higher education) and had experienced anxiety and confusion about this decision. He had discussed with friends, parents and educated people nearby in order to take a stream that would lead to a future job. Ravinder was experiencing a high level of confusion at the time of participating in the study. He was aiming for the military but had experienced several obstacles. He had enrolled for the entrance exam for the military, but his grade in Class 12 was too low to take the examination at pre-degree entry point. Moreover, he had been preparing for the army, but he was not tall enough (there is a minimum height restriction). He had taken the physical exam for the navy three times and had failed but was only one mark off. He was now going for the open admission to the army, which is less selective in terms of height and grades, and which therefore negated his ongoing higher education study. His back-up choice, like those mentioned earlier, was to become a teacher. He preferred a government job such as being a teacher to working for a private company as the workload is lighter and the salary is regular and fixed. As discussed earlier, his family was waiting to arrange his marriage, and he was trying to deter them. He also aspired to travel abroad and even to emigrate abroad with his parents, believing that emigration would bring good education and quick success. He was the only participant in our study to mention international travel. Narratives such as these show young men with a strong sense of their future family responsibility but accompanied by confusion about the best way to navigate their post-schooling options.

5.3 Conclusion

This chapter aimed to make visible the *silent comparator* that haunts many accounts of women's higher education access and choice – namely, men. The chapter set out masculine gender norms that, in a general sense, characterise many different societies, including within and beyond India. At the same time, the chapter described the nuances of the localised masculinity norms that characterise Haryana, showing the importance of digging down into contextual detail. In surfacing masculine gender norms, the relationality between masculine and feminine gender norms was exposed, including how this relationality shapes higher education access and choice differently for young men and young women.

Higher education in Haryana and in India is widely discussed in terms of honour and risk for young women. This chapter argues that men's lives are also shaped by concerns of honour and risk, but these notions are defined differently. Broadly, they are shaped by the expectation that they will assume lifelong responsibility for their parents and siblings, including material provision, physical presence and moral responsibility. For young men, their honour is bound up in taking responsibility for the family. An instrumental value is placed on having a son for this reason, and investments in sons are framed as lifetime investments rather than short-term, pre-marriage investments in women. Men are expected to stay within or close to the family home after marriage and to bring a bride to the home who will contribute labour and care. Importantly, marriage is not just associated with feminine norms – men are also expected to maintain or enhance their marriageability via financial stability and educational attainment, and as such spousal selection is a family affair, just as with women. Because men's honour is bound up in family responsibility, this means honour is not located within their bodies. Instead, their honour – and therefore the risk associated with their honour – is located within their futures, in particular, their potential to support the family. In this sense, men's spatial mobility is not restricted, and they are constructed as the unchastised perpetrators of various forms of sexual harassment, as long as they are preparing to provide for the family. This also means that trust takes a different form for young men. It is attached to the future – not to the body. As part of the notion of family responsibility, sons are expected to play a role in family decision making and in maintaining the reputation of the family. This includes surveilling and chaperoning their sisters and ensuring that their honour is protected. Importantly, this chapter included an example of a young woman who was acting as the son in her family, where there had been no surviving son of seven children, highlighting that masculine norms are not attached to men's bodies alone.

These notions of masculine honour and risk play out in various ways when it comes to higher education access and choice. Just as with women, decision making about men's higher education constitutes a spatial decision. In masculine norms, the spatial dimensions pertain to family responsibility.

One dimension relates to maintaining physical presence within the home, which necessitates choosing the nearest college or ensuring that at least one brother is at home. The second dimension concerns the responsibility to be aware of the household economy: young men were seen to choose a nearby government college to avoid draining family finances. Third, the future obligation of material provision entered into choice of institution, with young men weighing up the obligations of physical presence and financial responsibility sometimes contradicting the priority of accessing high quality higher education in order to make a greater financial contribution later on. Unlike with women, we saw that, for men, there were no concerns about the honour-related aspects of the *mahaul* or environment of the college, principally because men themselves constituted this *mahaul*. Arguably, spatial concerns of being at college did not affect men because higher education spaces are imbued with masculine tradition and therefore they feel more natural to men than women.

Enmeshed with spatial dimensions are the ways in which higher education access and choice intersect with masculine norms in different ways. For young men with lower levels of educational attainment in previous generations and a tradition of early contribution to the household economy, higher education could be seen as not enhancing or even as delaying the potential to enact family responsibility. This was layered with the social norms of masculinity in Haryana, where farming, sports and the military are often prized over academic achievements. Young men in these families were expected to either enrol in a shorter, vocational course or to start working upon the completion of high school. Higher education was also seen as a parallel activity to engage in alongside other – potentially more important – activities, with a degree seen as leading to a potential back-up option. In other families, higher education was seen as potentially enhancing a young man's potential to contribute to the family economy. Often this stemmed from previous generations' experiences of deprivation and economic struggle and a view that higher education would lead to social mobility. Included within this attitude was a curbing of men's freedom of course choice in that families were invested in their sons choosing a course with high employment prospects. Though less common for men than women, there was some evidence of young men being under pressure to marry quickly, and men resisting this during their higher education studies, but there was no evidence of men strategically accessing higher education *in order to* delay marriage. Finally, we saw a disconnect between higher education and employment aspirations for young men, though it was different to the disconnect that appeared in women's accounts. For young men, there seemed to be a confusion about the role higher education would play in their employment, and indeed how to shore up their futures as material providers in their families, given the lack of understanding within their families about graduate pathways and the multiple parallel strands of activity they were engaging in during their higher education studies.

In Chapter 4, we argued that attending higher education represented something of a gender transgression for young women, given the ways in which higher education challenges traditional norms of femininity. In this chapter, we have seen that, in some ways, higher education did not represent a transgression for young men in that it was often seen as a logical progression in educational attainment from the previous generation, and it did not challenge norms of spatial mobility. In other ways, higher education did represent a transgression, as it delayed men's ability to contribute to the household economy. Higher education also represented a risk, as families were often unsure if higher education would lead to employment. By looking directly at young men, talking to them and talking to young men about young women and vice versa, our study revealed two dominant constructions of masculinity, which are contradictory but should be seen together as completing the picture of how higher education access and choice are gendered. First, there is a sense of pervasive dehumanised masculinity, where public space – including journeys to college and college spaces – is characterised by masculine threat. In this construction, masculinity is collective, discursively represented as 'boys' and as abstract terms such as 'environment'. These young men are *other people's* sons and brothers; no one owned up to being or being related to these men. In the second construction, young men are constructed as earnestly building their futures and rather too assiduously protecting their sisters' honour; these young men are seen to be busying themselves with multiple strands of activity. These young men are *our* sons and brothers. These men must be the same men, with the same families, and all of them – and their families – are causing issues for young women. Yet, there seems to be a cultural split in the construction of masculinity, with young men held responsible for their own sisters but, for the most part, not made accountable for other people's sisters.

References

Adur, S. M., & Jha, S. (2018). (Re)centering street harassment – An appraisal of safe cities global initiative in Delhi, India. *Journal of Gender Studies, 27*(1), 114–124. https://doi.org/10.1080/09589236.2016.1264296

Agarwal, B. (1994). *Gender and command over property: An economic analysis of South Asia*. Kali for Women.

Bhog, D., & Mullick, D. (2015). *Collectivizing girls for social change: Strategies from India*. American Jewish World Service's Early and Child Marriage Initiative. Retrieved June 30, 2023, from https://ajws.org/our-impact/measuring-success/research-early-child-marriage/collectivizing-girls-for-social-change

Chanana, K. (2001). Hinduism and female sexuality: Social control and education of girls in India. *Sociological Bulletin, 50*(1), 37–63. https://doi.org/10.1177/0038022920010103

Chowdhry, P. (1986). The advantages of backwardness: Colonial policy and agriculture in Haryana. *The Indian Economic & Social History Review, 23*(3), 263–288. https://doi.org/10.1177/001946468602300302

Chowdhry, P. (1995). Contesting claims and counter-claims: Questions of the inheritance and sexuality of widows in a colonial state. *Contributions to Indian Sociology*, *29*(1–2), 65–82. https://doi.org/10.1177/0069966795029001005

Chowdhry, P. (1997). A matter of two shares: A daughter's claim to patrilineal property in rural North India. *The Indian Economic and Social History Review*, *34*(3), 289–320. https://doi.org/10.1177/001946469703400

Chowdhry, P. (1999). Ideology, culture and hierarchy: Expenditure-consumption patterns in rural households. In K. Sangari & U. Chakravarti (Eds.), *From myths to markets: Essays on gender* (pp. 274–311). Manohar Publishers and Distributors.

Chowdhry, P. (2004a). Caste panchayats and the policing of marriage in Haryana: Enforcing kinship and territorial exogamy. *Contributions to Indian Sociology*, *38*(1–2), 1–42. https://doi.org/10.1177/006996670403800102

Chowdhry, P. (2004b). Private lives, state intervention: Cases of runaway marriage in rural North India. *Modern Asian Studies*, *38*(1), 55–84. https://doi.org/10.1017/S0026749X04001027

Chowdhry, P. (2007). Fluctuating fortunes of wives: Creeping rigidity in inter-caste marriages in the colonial period. *Indian Historical Review*, *34*(1), 210–243. https://doi.org/10.1177/037698360703400

Gautam, M. (2015). Gender, subject choice and higher education in India: Exploring "choices" and "constraints" of women students. *Contemporary Education Dialogue*, *12*(1), 31–58. https://doi.org/10.1177/0973184914556865

Husain, Z., & Sarkar, S. (2011). Gender disparities in educational trajectories in India: Do females become more robust at higher levels? *Social Indicators Research*, *101*(1), 37–56.

Narwana, K., & Gill, A. S. (2020). Beyond access and inclusion: Dalit experiences of participation in higher education in rural Punjab. *Contemporary Voice of Dalit*, *12*(2), 234–248. https://doi.org/10.1177/2455328X20925592

Oza, R. (2019). Wrestling women: Caste and neoliberalism in rural Haryana. *Gender, Place & Culture*, *26*(4), 468–488. https://doi.org/10.1080/0966369X.2018.1502162

Panchal, T. J., Thusoo, S., & Ajgaonkar, V. (2020). Child marriages in Haryana: Challenges in implementing PCMA, 2006. *Economic and Political Weekly*, *55*(19), 58–64.

Thomas, A. (2021). *The role of families in the gendered educational trajectories of undergraduate students in Haryana, India* [Unpublished PhD dissertation]. University of Warwick.

6 Conclusion

6.1 Introduction

This book began with two interrelated questions: Why do young people from the same families and communities experience different decision-making processes about their educational futures? Why are different gendered decisions taken about applying for higher education? Posing these questions is vital at a point in time where many higher education systems are reaching gender parity of enrolment in undergraduate education, and women's enrolment is even exceeding men's in many country contexts. Just because gender parity has been reached does not mean that gender disappears. Societies are still for the most part organised along binary gendered lines, based on the expectations of heterosexual marriage between cis-gendered individuals. This means that, while gendered norms and expectations may shift over time, gender surfaces in new ways, both in terms of normative codes and transgressive possibilities. Gender parity may have been reached, but this does not mean that people of different genders stand shoulder to shoulder at the gates of higher education institutions, with the same histories behind them and the same ideas about higher education in their minds.

In this chapter, we first return to the initial premise of the book set out in Chapter 1 to chart the journey that the chapters have taken through an analysis of gendered higher education access and choice in the massification generation in India. Second, we set out considerations for policy strategy and further research, in terms of how the arguments presented in the book could be deployed to change actions as well as minds. Third, the chapter specifically returns to the gendered focus of the book, arguing that the book has served as an exemplification of how gender analysis in this field can be conducted, and why a nuanced, holistic gender analysis is so necessary in understanding higher education access and choice. Finally, the chapter concludes with a reminder that, due to the evolving nature of both gender and higher education, the questions addressed in the book are not resolved and will always need to be discussed and re-discussed.

6.2 Gendering the massification generation

Each substantive chapter of this book (Chapters 2–5) has added to a cumulative picture of higher education access and choice as a gendered phenomenon in Haryana, in India and beyond. This section presents a synthesis of the key arguments of the book from the four substantive chapters.

A vital starting point for the book was to conduct an analysis of the characteristics of the massification generation in India, particularly those young people accessing higher education from relatively disadvantaged communities. The term 'massification generation' refers to the entrants to higher education during the era where a higher education system expands substantially. The nature and meaning of higher education change during the massification process, and so-called 'new entrants' to higher education bring ideas and ideals with them about what higher education will involve and what it will bring in terms of future benefits. Chapter 2 was set in this context. The chapter deliberately followed in the footsteps of much of the research in this area by focusing on indicators of social disadvantage and eliding gender issues. Characteristics of the massification generation included being of the first generation in the family to access higher education; substantial 'leaps' in educational attainment between grandparents, parents and then the young people of the massification generation; lack of experience of graduate-level employment in previous generations; reliance on other members of the massification generation for information about higher education choices and processes; living local lives; depending on walking and public transport; a school record of attending government schools (with education delivered in Hindi, in this context) and/or switching between government and private schools according to family finances and priorities. The chapter discussed that young people from marginalised groups were more likely to experience intensified forms of disadvantage in relation to higher education access and choice.

While Chapter 2 set out a convincing set of common characteristics of the massification generation, Chapter 3 created a cleavage in this homogenised picture by introducing a first layer of gender analysis. This analysis involved disaggregating the data presented in Chapter 2 by gender, showing a different set of characteristics for young women and young men from the massification generation. Overall, the chapter showed that, even if daughters and sons from the same families and communities are arriving together at the gates of higher education, they are arriving with different expectations placed on them and different experiences behind them. For daughters, by accessing higher education, they were more likely to be making a huge generational leap in terms of educational attainment. They were also pushing at gender norms by aspiring to formal employment after higher education. Daughters were living more local lives than their brothers, and attending higher education signified breaking significant spatial boundaries placed on young women's spatial mobility.

Moreover, daughters were attending higher education having accessed less costly and reputedly lower quality schooling than their brothers, with less access to education in English. For young men, on the other hand, they were following a stepped pattern of educational attainment from previous generations, where higher education was the logical next step. Graduate employment was also a logical next step in terms of a family's expectations of social mobility resting on their son/s. Sons were living local lives but with fewer restrictions and perceived risks than their sisters. They received investment in their schooling to the extent of their families' capacities and, therefore, also were more likely than their sisters to access some education in English. From Chapter 3, a contextually nuanced picture of gender difference within the massification generation in Haryana not only appeared but also revealed general principles that could be applied more generally to India and beyond.

While Chapter 3 exploded the notion of a homogenous massification generation, Chapters 4 and 5 focused on the next level of gender analysis, unpacking the gender norms attached to femininity and masculinity. Chapter 4 addressed gender norms attached to femininity, and how these feed into higher education access and choice. While the gender disaggregation analysis presents gender difference as a fact, the analysis of femininity reveals the underpinnings – gender norms – that serve to solidify expectations about what is right and proper for young women and that come to act as normalised explanations for gender difference. While the gender norms explored in the chapter were heavily contextualised in the Haryana context, basic principles from these norms have wider salience. The chapter first set out dominant gender norms associated with femininity – namely, the notion that an unmarried woman's honour is also the family's honour and that a woman's future is characterised by marriage as her main purpose and action. The chapter then explored how these norms play into decisions about higher education access and choice. In terms of honour, the protection of an unmarried woman's honour is a family project and risk prevention is the major strategy. This feeds into restricted access to higher education and limited choice. Higher education can be seen as a risk to marriageability – 'too much' education – or a neutral means of waiting for marriage – 'time pass' – or a positive or even required asset to make a good match. A parallel discourse appeared in the analysis of young women aspiring to post-higher education employment. Overall, the chapter revealed that higher education may be highly confusing for massification generation families, who are navigating the fact that simply attending a nearby higher education institution in and of itself represents a transgression of femininity, based on customary gender norms.

Chapter 5 presented the partner chapter for Chapter 4, exploring underpinnings of masculinity in relation to higher education access and choice. This chapter also represented an important intervention in the gender analysis landscape, as many studies of gendered higher education access focus on women's lives only, meaning that analyses of masculinity are highly neglected in this area, and men serve as a *silent comparator*. Given the relationality between women's and men's lives in a society organised around norms of heterosexual marriage, it was a key argument of this chapter that an understanding of masculine norms is vital in order to piece together an understanding of gender inequalities. Again, this chapter not only was 'firmly rooted in gender norms of Haryana but also pointed to more widespread norms that are applicable across India and beyond. As with feminine gender norms, the chapter revealed that masculinity also rests on ideals of family honour; however, honour for young men has a different meaning, and therefore risk to honour is also characterised in a different manner. For young men, there is an assumption that sons will take up lifelong responsibility for their parents and siblings, along the lines of financial provision, physical presence and moral responsibility. In terms of higher education access and choice, this was layered with notions of family responsibility, including choosing the nearest college to maintain physical presence or not to drain family finances, or selecting a college that would bring the most financial returns for the future, and enhancing marriageability. Higher education was associated with risk in the sense of fears about the translation of a degree into employment prospects, and many young men were engaged in multiple strands of activity such as coaching for military or administrative service exams or sports training, where higher education was just one strand of their lives and potentially just represented a 'plan B'. While higher education represented less of a transgression for young men in terms of norms of masculinity, there were still elements of transgression caused by the delay to becoming a fully-fledged contributor to the family economy.

Moving through these four steps of gender analysis showed the deep intertwining of gender norms with higher education and choice. Facing up to this nuance and complexity is essential in order to contemplate forms of social transformation that recognise how gender norms operate, rather than skimming over the surface of gender difference.

6.3 Implications for policy strategy and further research

A first implication of the evidence presented in this book is that gender inequalities play out in many different ways and that questions need to be asked in an enduring manner about gendered higher education access and choice. For instance if young women are outnumbering young men in undergraduate education, does this mean that young men think they have found a better option than higher education and that young women have not yet caught up? Or that expectations of employment for young men are not being satisfied by higher education qualifications, and young women are engaging in higher education for 'time pass' as they await marriage? Gender will never be solved or resolved, as gendered roles and expectations – and transgressions – are in constant evolution and flux, with new forms of progressive and conservative femininity and masculinity always emerging. *A first implication, therefore is: retain a focus* on gender in policy strategy and in future research, taking parity as a cue for further research rather than as an end point.

It is important to recognise that higher education represents a transgression of norms of femininity – in terms of appropriate educational and spatial limits – as otherwise it can be tempting to try to persuade families to send their daughters to higher education using misplaced arguments. Where the resistance is rooted in fear, making arguments for change based on recognising a woman's intrinsic worth or economic potential run the risk of missing the mark. What families need is reassurance. However, many strategies designed to reassure are deeply embedded in and therefore reinforcing of gender norms, such as distance education that means a woman can stay at home and women's colleges with dedicated bus services that keep women cloistered away from men. Much harder is to find means of reassurance that are rooted in challenging the climate of compromise and constraint that characterises women's higher education access and choice. We believe that one such strategy is to open the doors of colleges to prospective students and their families, as with the 'taster days' we have trialled where students and their families can visit the premises (Samanta et al., 2022, see also Appendix A), to debunk rumours of co-educational colleges as hotbeds of youthful misdemeanour. *A second implication, therefore, is: scope out reasons for resistance to gender equality in higher education access and choice and design strategies that target this resistance, rather than assuming where the resistance comes from and/or designing strategies that reinforce limiting gender norms.*

In addition to representing transgression, higher education also represents risk. In the dominant framing of masculinity, higher education specifically represents a risk to potential future earning potential, given common mistrust of the graduate employment market. In this scenario, further provision of reliable information about degree courses and career options would be of benefit in terms of family reassurance and the opening up of young people's trajectories. In young women's accounts, a sense emerged of employment aspirations that were nascent and seemingly at odds with the expectations of their families and their future in-laws. For young men, it appeared that they were often engaged in parallel activities to shore up their futures, meaning that higher education was just one of a number of activities, and therefore was not valued as an experience in and of itself, with attrition and patchy attendance being common phenomena. *A third implication, therefore, is: consider the role of higher education in young people's potential employment prospects, conduct further research on shifting aspirations and norms around femininity-higher education-employment and masculinity-higher education-employment and embed more pathway planning into guidance about higher education choice.*

These are just three areas where concrete implications have emerged from the analysis conducted for this book. Many more recommendations and considerations are presented in the open access resources published from the research on Haryana (see Appendix A).

6.4 Furthering gender analysis of higher education access and choice

In addition to the implications for policy strategy and further research presented in the previous section, this book has demonstrated a nuanced, holistic gender analysis of higher education access and choice, with the aim of providing an exemplar for future research in this domain, across country contexts. The book has walked readers through a social disadvantage analysis (Chapter 2), a gender disaggregation process (Chapter 3), a deeper analysis focusing on norms of femininity (Chapter 4) and a complementary analysis of masculinity norms (Chapter 5). There is still an argument for using gender disaggregation analysis, as a hallmark of feminist development thought, provided that as many genders as are present are included in the analysis. Chapters 4 and 5 served as an important reminder that gender disaggregation in itself does not suffice, as it runs the risk of reinforcing deterministic messaging about gender difference being the explanation of gender inequality. Gender difference does not in and of itself explain gender inequality; for this, a contextually nuanced exploration of gender norms is needed. Inherent to this exploratory process is the identification of both *norms* and *transgressions*. It is necessary to consider how codes of femininity and masculinity attach to different gendered bodies, objects and practices, meaning that femininity is not restricted to women, and masculinity is not confined to men. While the analysis presented in this book often focused on a tightknit association between women and femininity, and men and masculinity, we have tried to consistently remind readers that, *where there are gender norms, there is gender transgression, and in gender transgression lies the potential for social transformation.*

In establishing a careful process of gender analysis that other researchers in this area could follow, we have travelled far from the absent or basic gender analyses that dominate the field of higher education access research. However, this does not mean that we have reached the end of possibilities. Far from it. Greater cross-pollination between gender studies research and research on higher education access and choice would be highly beneficial to extend the current landscape of research (Henderson, 2019). More is needed to understand how the full range of gender identities and affinities play out in making choices about higher education. We already have evidence from studies conducted in India of challenges faced by transgender students in the admissions process (Mary, 2023) and of the sheer impossibility of reaching higher levels of study for young queer-identifying people who are banished from their families upon coming out (Shah et al., 2015). There is a growing attention on people choosing to be single, including in Indian scholarship (Chowkhani & Wynne, 2024), and this trend surely intersects with higher education decision making. We hope that this book can provide a foundation for more nuanced, holistic analyses of gendered higher education access and choice, while also serving as a springboard for further important work exploring neglected intricacies of gender in Indian society and beyond.

6.5 Final thoughts

At the core of this volume has been an exploration of how young people from the same families and communities experience different decision-making processes about higher education. This exploration has led us through, in particular, how gender parity indices mask disparities between young women and men in preparation for higher education, choice about higher education options and expectations about the outcomes of higher education. While society operates along profoundly gendered lines, these disparities will remain in some form or other. Why does it matter so much that we retain a focus on an issue that many have declared solved? While higher education retains even something of its status as a key phase in the educational trajectory, as a vehicle for social mobility and as an opportunity for personal and social growth, it also retains its status as a site where equalities and/or inequalities play out – in terms of who can enter which institution, where and to study what. While there are young people whose ascribed gender shapes their higher education access and choice – and their future lives and who they can be as people – in a way that reproduces deep and unfair gender norms, this work deserves sustained attention.

References

Chowkhani, K., & Wynne, C. (2024). *Singular selves: An introduction to single studies*. Routledge India.

Henderson, E. F. (2019). Starting with gender: Definitional politics in international higher education research. In E. F. Henderson & Z. Nicolazzo (Eds.), *Starting with gender in international higher education research: Conceptual debates and methodological considerations* (pp. 12–28). Routledge.

Mary, S. A. (2023). Structural marginalisation of transgender students in higher education institutions of India. In K. Kikhi & D. R. Gautam (Eds.), *Marginality in India: Perspectives of marginalisation from the Northeast* (pp. 110–126). Routledge India.

Samanta, N., Thomas, A., Mansuy, J., Stewart, A., Henderson, E. F., & Sabharwal, N. S. (2022). *Fair chance for education outreach activity resource for higher education institutions: Organising a college visit "taster day" for potential higher education applicants*. University of Warwick.

Shah, C., Merchant, R., Mahajan, S., & Nevatia, S. (2015). *No outlaws in the gender galaxy*. Zubaan.

Appendix A
The 'Fair Chance for Education' project

This book is based on empirical data collected during Phase 1 of a five-year research project entitled *Fair Chance for Education: Gendered Pathways to Educational Success in Haryana*, which was funded by the Fair Chance Foundation. Further information and project outputs can be located via the project website: www.warwick.ac.uk/haryana).

More information about the Phase 1 study can be found in the Phase 1 report:

- **Phase 1:** Henderson, E. F., Thomas, A., Mansuy, J., Sabharwal, N. S., Stewart, A., Rathee, S., Yadav, R., & Samanta, N. (2021). *A fair chance for education: Gendered pathways to educational success in Haryana: Phase 1 findings report*. Retrieved September 10, 2023, from University of Warwick. https://wrap.warwick.ac.uk/155467/

Phase 1 was followed by two funded doctoral studies which constituted Phase 2, which focused on the role of the family in higher education access, and Phase 3, which focused on the role of government colleges in higher education access. More information can be located in the reports:

- **Phase 2:** Thomas, A., & Henderson, E. F. (2022). *A fair chance for education: Gendered pathways to educational success in Haryana. Phase 2 report: The role of families in the gendered educational trajectories of undergraduate students in Haryana, India*. University of Warwick. Retrieved September 10, 2023, from https://wrap.warwick.ac.uk/170400/
- **Phase 3:** Samanta, N., & Stewart, A. (2023). *Phase 3 report: Institutional initiatives to support informed choice in accessing higher education: Implementing a taster day in government colleges in Haryana, India*. University of Warwick. Retrieved September 10, 2023, from https://wrap.warwick.ac.uk/175560/

Appendix A

Phase 4 of the study involved enhancing the social impact of the project and resulted in a policy brief and an 'Outreach Activity Resource' to assist colleges with implementing an open day or taster day for prospective students and their families to visit the colleges. The activities are reported on in more detail in the Phase 4 report:

- **Policy Brief:** Stewart, A., Henderson, E. F., Sabharwal, N. S., Thomas, A., Samanta, N., & Mansuy, J. (2022). *Supporting gender-sensitive higher education access and choice in Haryana, India: Policy Brief*. University of Warwick. Retrieved September 10, 2023, from https://wrap.warwick.ac.uk/167420/
- **Outreach Activity Resource:** Samanta, N., Thomas, A., Mansuy, J., Stewart, A., Henderson, E. F., & Sabharwal, N. S. (2022). *Fair chance for education outreach activity resource for higher education institutions: Organising a college visit "taster day" for potential higher education applicants*. University of Warwick. Retrieved September 10, 2023, from https://wrap.warwick.ac.uk/167421/
- **Phase 4:** Stewart, A., Mansuy, J., & Thomas, A. (2023). *Phase 4 report: The contribution to educational policy development of the fair chance for education research on gendered access to higher education*. University of Warwick. Retrieved September 10, 2023, from https://wrap.warwick.ac.uk/175562/

The final project report which brings together the aforementioned outputs is also available.

- **Final Report:** Stewart, A., Henderson, E. F., Mansuy, J., Thomas, A., Samanta, N., Sabharwal, N. S., Rathee, S., & Yadav, R. (2023). *A fair chance for education: Gendered pathways to educational success in Haryana. Final project report*. University of Warwick. Retrieved September 10, 2023, from https://wrap.warwick.ac.uk/175226/

The project was supported by a Research Advisory Group consisting of experts in the areas of gender and education, and a Consultative Group of early career researchers, and was designed following the team's engagement with a commissioned literature review presentation by two of the project partners, Nandini Manjrekar and Manish Jain:

- Manjrekar, N., & Jain, M. (2016, September 30). *Social context of girls education in Haryana* [Unpublished literature review presentation, fair chance foundation scoping meeting]. Habitat Centre, New Delhi.

The authors of this book, in order, took the following roles in the project, and all have contributed to the production of the book:

- Emily F. Henderson – Co-Investigator and Lead of Phase 1
- Nidhi S. Sabharwal – Project Partner
- Anjali Thomas – PhD Scholar and then Post-Doctoral Fellow and Lead of Phase 2 with Henderson
- Julie Mansuy – Project Coordinator
- Ann Stewart – Principal Investigator, Lead of Phase 3 with Samanta, Lead of Phase 4
- Sharmila Rathee – Member of Consultative Group and Phase 1 Fieldwork Coordinator
- Renu Yadav – Member of Consultative Group and Phase 1 Fieldwork Coordinator
- Nikita Samanta – PhD Scholar and Lead of Phase 3

Appendix B
Details of the participants and survey sample

Participant information for the qualitative study

Table A.1 Student Interview Participant Basic Information

College	Pseudonym	Gender	Age (years)	Caste group	Religion	Course	Place of residence
SDC	Rajvi	Woman	21	General	Hindu	BA	Village c. 10 km from SDC urban centre
SDC	Neetu	Woman	19	General	Hindu	BSc	SDC urban centre
SDC	Ravinder	Man	20	General	Hindu	BA	Village c. 10 km from SDC urban centre
SDC	Sachin	Man	20	OBC	Hindu	BSc	Village c. 10 km from SDC urban centre
MDC	Rajni	Woman	23	General	Hindu	BA	MDC urban centre
MDC	Seema	Woman	18	SC	Hindu	BSc	Village c. 20 km from SDC urban centre
MDC	Vikas	Man	19	OBC	Hindu	BCom	Near to the college [further information not recorded]
MDC	Amit	Man	21	OBC	Hindu	BCom	Village [further information not recorded]

Source: authors.

Appendix B 109

Table A.2 Student FGD Participant Basic Information

College	Gender	Pseudonyms	Course	Age (years)	Caste group	Religion
SDC	Women	Babli, Kavita, Kusum, Manisha, Ritu	BCom	19–21	3 × General 1 × BCB 1 × BCA	4 × Hindu 1 × Jain
SDC	Men	Mandeep, Naresh, Rahul, Sanjay, Satish	BCom	17–20	2 × General 2 × BCB 1 × SC	4 × Hindu 1 × Hindu/Jain
MDC	Women	Kamna, Neha, Neela, Poonam, Reena	(Not noted by research assistant)	17–18	2 × General 1 × BCB 1 × BCA 1 × BC (A/B unspecified)	5 × Hindu
MDC	Men	Harish, Jatin, Kaushal, Parvesh, Sunil	2 × BCom 3 × BA	16–20	1 × General 1 × BCA 1 × BC (A/B unspecified) 1 × SC 1 × caste group unspecified	5 × Hindu

Source: authors.

Table A.3 College Representative Interviews Participant Basic Information

College	Position	Gender
MDC	Associate professor (senior status)	Man
SDC	Associate professor (senior status)	Man

Source: authors.

Survey sample information

Table A.4 Survey Sample Information: By College and Overall

	Overall sample	MDC	SDC	SiDC
Sample	326	124	118	84
Gender	Women: 42.1%	Women: 16%	Women: 66.4%	Women: 47.6%
Note 1: % of valid responses	Men: 57.9%	Men: 84%	Men: 33.6%	Men: 52.4%
Note 2: No respondents specified genders other than women/man		Note: college data revealed 12% women, 88% men	Note: college data revealed 62% women, 38% men	Note: college data revealed 20% women, 80% men, but the accuracy of this data was questionable
Caste group	General: 36.1%	General: 25.4%	General: 57.5%	General: 21.5%
Note 1: % of valid responses	BCB: 19.7%	BCB: 39%	BCB: 11.5%	BCB: 2.5%
Note 2: 'General' indicates not belonging to BCB, BCA, SC or Scheduled Tribes.	BCA: 20%	BCA: 16.9%	BCA: 18.6%	BCA: 26.6%
	SC: 24.2%	SC: 18.6%	SC: 12.4%	SC: 49.4%
				Note: Sirsa district has the second highest proportion of SC in Haryana at 29.9%, as shown in Census 2011.
Religion	Hindus: 97.5%	Hindus: 100%	Hindus: 98.2%	Hindus: 92.9%
Note: % of valid responses	Christians: 0.3%	Note: Mahendragarh district has 99% Hindus according to Census 2011.	Christians: 0.9%	Sikhs: 7.1%
	Jains: 0.3%		Jains: 0.9%	Note: Sirsa district has 72.6% Hindus and 26.17 Sikhs according to Census 2011.
	Sikhs: 1.9%		Note: Sonipat district has 95.9% Hindus according to Census 2011.	
Course being studied	BSc: 30.9%	BSc: 56.5%	BSc: 28.9%	BSc (not available)
Note: % of valid responses	BCom: 33.2%	BCom: 36.1%	BCom: 43.9%	BCom: 14.6%
	BA: 35.9%	BA: 7.4%	BA: 27.2%	BA: 85.4%

Source: authors.

Note: MDC, SDC, SiDC are pseudonyms.

Appendix B 111

Further particulars on the study procedure and data analysis

- The study was granted ethical approval from the appropriate University of Warwick ethics committee.
- The study design and instruments were developed in consultation across the project partners, and three members of the Consultative Group (Sharmila Rathee, Manju Panwar, Roma Smart Joseph) tested the instruments with their students.
- Along with the team members listed in the authorship group, data collection was conducted by three doctoral scholar research assistants who were trained by the team before embarking on fieldwork (Sooraj H.S., Annu Kumari, Sohan Lal). The questionnaire was presented in a bilingual format of English and Hindi, and the majority of the interviews were conducted in Hindi. The audio files were transcribed by a doctoral scholar research assistant (Somak) and translated in a bilingual format by Anjali Thomas. The quantitative survey data was entered into SPSS and cleaned and checked and then descriptively analysed.
- The qualitative survey data was coded and re-entered into SPSS as new coded variables.
- A student profile was developed from each student interview to give a holistic picture of each participant, including demographic information; marital status/plans; family background; schooling; higher education access/choice process; admissions' experience; journey to college; future aspirations; social discourses evoked (e.g. culture, politics).
- The college representative interviews, student interviews and student FGDs were also thematically analysed in relation to key aspects of higher education access and choice (e.g. college choice, family background).
- This process also included a data analysis workshop with the book co-authors to guide the process and a comprehensive bilingual reading of the transcripts by Emily F. Henderson and Nikita Samanta. The data were re-read with a specific gender lens in view of the prevalent gender norms in Haryana (see Section 1.4) to produce the analyses for this book.

Index

Note: Page numbers in *italic* indicate a figure and page numbers in **bold** indicate a table on the corresponding page.

access 103–104; and femininity 57–62, 64–65, 67–74, 76–77; and masculinity 80–81, 83–86, 88–89, 91, 93–96
admissions process 4–6, 24, 31, 91–93, 103
analytical approach 10–12

barriers 73–74

caste 1–4, 9, 13–14, 26–7, 35–7, 45–8, *45*, 68
choice 103–104
Chowdhry, Prem 10, 13, 45, 48–50, 58–59, 68, 81–84, 88
Class 12 6–7, 36, 66–69, 88–89
colonial legacy 2–3
commutability 30–33, *31–32*; gendering 50–51
commuting as risky 61–67, *65*

district 15, 29–33, 37, 66, 72, 86–87

education: gendering previous generations 41–49, *44–45*; grandparents 26; parents 27–28; previous generations 22–29
empirical study 15–16
employability 81–84
employment: and family responsibility 92–93; gendering previous generations 41–49, *44–45*; and marriageability 74–75; previous generations 22–29

Fair Chance for Education 105–107
family 67–69, 80–81, 94–96; employability and marriage 81–84; and higher education 85–93
father 41–42, 45–49, *45*, 54, 89, 91
femininity/ies 57–58, 76–77; commuting to and studying at college as risky endeavors 61–67, *65*; honour, safety and risk 58–60; intersections between higher education and marriageability 69–75; marriage, family and investment 67–69

gender 7–10
gender analysis 41–42, 103–104
gender disaggregation 10–11, 40, 53, 55, 100, 103
gender inequality/ies 1–2, 9, 43, 77, 101, 103
gendering 40–41, 53–55, 99–101; massification generation 49–53, *52*; previous generations 41–49, *44–45*
gender lens 2, 10, 40, 42, 44, 111
gender norms 2, 11–16, 94, 100–104
gender parity 8–10, 40, 42, 54, 98, 104
Gender Parity Index (GPI) 8, 14
generations *see* massification generation; previous generations
GER *see* Gross Enrolment Ratio (GER)
government college 1–7, *6–7*, 15, 27–30, 33–37, 49–50, 63–65, *65*, 85–87

GPI *see also* Gender Parity Index (GPI)
grandparents, grandmother, grandfather 25–27, 36–37, 41–46, *44*, 54, 89
Gross Enrolment Ratio (GER) 3, 8, 14

Haryana 99–102; 1–2, *6–7*, 11–15; *Fair Chance for Education* project 105–106; femininity 57–60, 64–68, 73–77; gendering 42–44, 47–50, 53–55; masculinity 80–81, 88–90, 94–95; massification generation 22, 25–26, 29–34, *31–32*, 37
higher education 103–104; femininity 57–79; and gender in India 7–10; in India 2–7, *6–7*; and marriage 67–76; masculinity 80–97; as risk for young men 81–93; as risk for young women 58–67
histories of schooling 33–36, *35*, 51–53, *52*
honour/*izzat* 58–67

India: gender and higher education in 7–10; higher education in 2–7, *6–7*
investment in education 67–69

knowledge of previous generations 25, 42

local lives 30–33, *31–32*; gendering 50–51

marriage 11–13, 42–43, 50, 58–59, 61, 76–77, 94–98, 100–101; family and investment 67–69; family responsibility 81–84; intersections between higher education and 69–75; and masculine family responsibility 85–93
marriageability: and family responsibility 81–84; and higher education 69–75
masculinity/ies 1–2, 67, 80–81, 94–96, 100–103; family responsibility 81–93

massification generation 21–22, 29–37, 40–41, 53–55, 99–101; gendering 49–53; and previous generations 22–29, 41–49
medium of instruction (MoI) 34–37, 53–54
mother 41–49, *45*, 54, 71–75, 89–91

parents: education 27–28; employment 28–29; gendering education 44–47, *45*; gendering employment 47–49
participants of the research study **108–110**, 111
policy strategy 101–102
previous generations: education and employment 22–29; gendering 41–49, *44–45*

responsibility 81–82, 84–95, 101
risk: for young men 81–93; for young women 58–67, *65*
rural 14–15, 30–32, 35–37, 53–54

safety 58–67, *65*
school choice 8–9, 99–100; and femininity 57, 69–71; gendering 50–56; and masculinity 86, 93–95; massification generation 22–27, 30, 34–37
schooling histories 33–36, *35*; gendering 51–53, *52*
sex ratio 13
son preference 49–50, 52–54, 81, 83
studying at college as risky 61–67, *65*
survey sample **108–110**, 111

'time pass' 76, 90, 100–101; and young men 90; and young women 70–71
transport 33, 37, 50–51, 54–55, 62–63, 85–87, 99

urban 15–16, 30–32, 35–37, 51–54, 66, 85–87

widening participation 1, 5

For Product Safety Concerns and Information please contact our EU representative GPSR@taylorandfrancis.com
Taylor & Francis Verlag GmbH, Kaufingerstraße 24, 80331 München, Germany